NEW & COLLECTED
Poems & Images

Lindsay Rabbitt

NEW & COLLECTED
Poems & Images

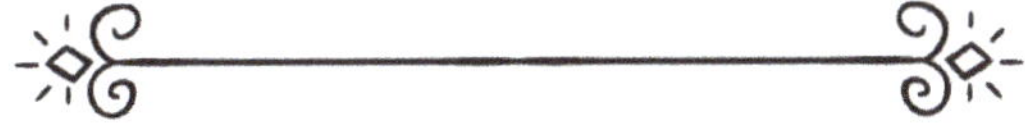

EDITED BY
Mike Johnson

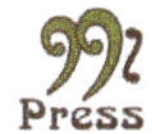
Press

Published by 99% Press
an imprint of Lasavia Publishing Ltd.
Auckland, New Zealand
www.lasaviapublishing.com
in association with
Voice Press
Raumati, Aotearoa New Zealand
www.lindsay@lindsayrabbitt.com

Copyright ©Lindsay Rabbitt, 2024
Drawings © Jane Pountney; Bodhi Vincent
Photos © Lindsay Rabbitt
Typographic images © Lindsay Rabbitt
Cover design: Lindsay Rabbitt
Computer rendering: Jeff Simmonds
Book design: Daniela Gast

Front cover photo (a nod to Magritte): the poet at the
Surrealists exhibition, Museum of New Zealand Te Papa, 2021.
Back cover photo: the poet, 1985, locking up a chase (aka a form)
of movable type for letterpress printing.

ISBN: 978-1-991083-18-0

In Memory of

Jane Elizabeth Pountney
Artist & Teacher
1949 – 2004

&

Gordon Eric Aimers
Artist
1925 – 2008

Contents

Introduction
Cutting to the Chase

heh, he's just got
the bare facts, eh

For Lindsay Rabbitt, poetry is no decorative art, no fancy words for the sake of fancy words. It doesn't set out to prettify anything; it is essential, irreducible language. A no-frills poetic, it has its own brute music. It doesn't mess about trying to be flashy and impress the impressionable, or put on any verbal fireworks. Through a process of elimination and honing, we arrive at some essential truth or understanding, a poem built from little blocks of language that cannot be pared down any further, separated by plenty of space to let in light and mind.

For Lindsay Rabbitt, words are like physical objects. You can rub up against them. It began that way as the young Lindsay learned typesetting and typography as a craft and a job. In this day of cyber words and computer printing, it's worthwhile reminding ourselves of just what this ancient craft, going back to Guttenburg, involved. It involves typefaces, point sizes, line lengths, line spacing and letter spacing.

Wikipedia describes typesetting thus:

'During much of the letterpress era movable type was composed by hand for each page by workers called compositors. A tray with many dividers, called a case, contained cast metal *sorts*, each with a single letter or symbol, but backwards (so they would print correctly). The compositor assembled these sorts into words, then lines, then pages of text, which were then bound tightly together by a frame, making up a *form* or page. If done correctly, all letters were of the same height, and a flat surface of type was created. The form was placed in a press and inked, and then printed (an impression made) on paper. Metal type read backwards, from right to left, and a key skill of the compositor was their ability to read this backwards text.' The picture shows movable typeface on a composing stick sitting on a tray.

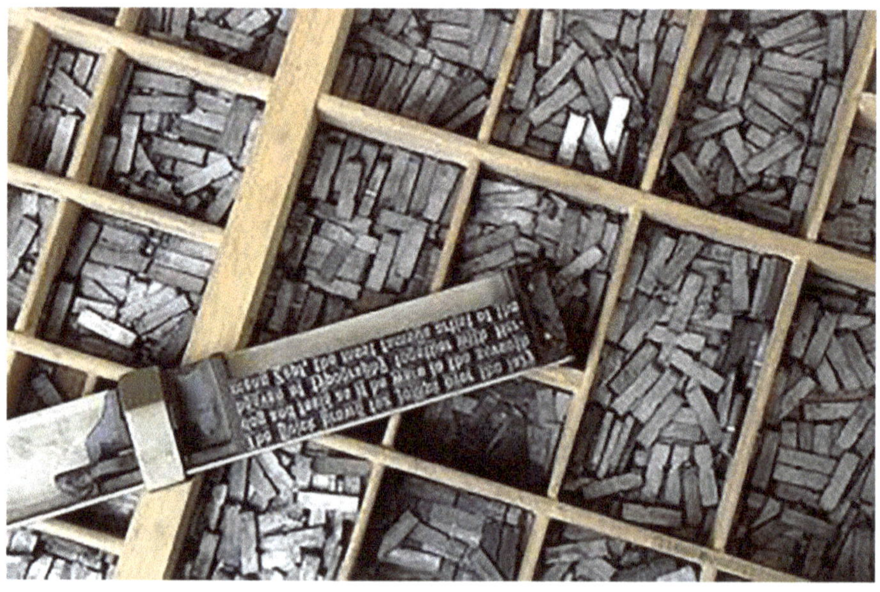

So, for the compositor Lindsay, words were not *like* physical objects, they were, literally, physical objects – letters, moulded on pieces of lead, and assembled by hand in a setting stick; later, mechanically, on a linotype keyboard. This slow and exacting process became the basis of Lindsay Rabbitt's aesthetic. Words and blocks of words are *placed* in spatial relation to each other. Meanings jostle, sounds rub up against each other. When read aloud the words take on the physicality of voice, blocks of sound assembled with a bricklayer's care, sonic objects in themselves. 'Lindsay Rabbitt's poetry works well as pure cadence, quite apart from meaning,' Bill Manhire says in a 1985 review of *On The Line* in Wellington City Magazine.

In an email to me, Lindsay commented, 'Because I handset type, individual letters and words became physical materials to make pre-press posters and fruit box labels etc. Then when I set copy on a linotype the sound of the machine and the way I received clusters of words as I typed them instilled the rhythm or cadence of language.'

This results in gnomic, durable utterances of revelatory power. The poems are not so much about things but are in themselves things, the closest we can come in poetry to Kant's *ding an sich* – the thing-in-itself. 'They read like proverbs, enigmatic I Ching announcements, hilltop meditations upon the true and insignificant,' Ian Wedde wrote in a 1988 Evening Post review of Jane Pountney's multi-panelled charcoal work *Towards a Landscape* (exhibited at the Southern Cross Gallery, Wellington) in which Lindsay Rabbitt's poem 'a way' from *thewayofit* was imbedded.

Such poems are not so much a commentary on the world but an uncovering of the shape of things as perceived. And what may be uncovered is not so much a 'thing' necessarily but a movement, a sudden emergence. The purity of Euclidean geometry is interrupted by the abrupt emergence of life:

the line
is the lie

the world
is

the world
is flat/

allofasudden
a tree stands

up straight

We can make a useful distinction between what words say and what they do, between their descriptive and performative aspects. While words will always mean something, carry some freight of significance, Lindsay Rabbitt's poetry is constantly pivoting away from meaning and towards performance. These poems do not describe but enact: they are enactments celebrating the power of words to bring things into being rather than describe things already known and settled. These poems are unsettling because they do not take the world for granted but discover it, emergent, in the process of the writing. A moment captured.

It is not just the outer world which is disclosed/brought into being in such a way but the 'self,' the personality, the inner self, and here we find a shifting world of feelings and a certain flinty humour.

my face is
there in the mirror

looks as if
I don't belong to it

looks at me looks

looks as if
it wants approval

A beautifully precise and droll way of expressing that dissociation from self that we experience when looking in a mirror.

We have to negotiate the world of abstractions in the same way we do with the world of objects:

simple works/just well

This minimalism is reminiscent of Robert Creeley, who had a big influence on New Zealand poetry in the 1980s when Lindsay started publishing, but the poems are very much their own voice, the ineluctable voice of Lindsay Rabbitt, a voice fully aware of what it's doing, the nature of this paring back, this uncovering:

i set about
to weed

the garden

till all i see
is black earth

Given the spare nature of his verse, it's not surprising that his overall output of poetry has been small. Like precious jewels they have a rarity value. We have three 'little books' in the 1980s and the more extensive *Prayers for the Living & the Dead* in 2021. In that almost thirty-year gap, Lindsay was working with graphic designs some of which are included in this book. From morpheme to grapheme was a natural movement for Lindsay.

The three 'little books,' as Lindsay and I began to call them when discussing this collection, were *upagainstit*, 1983, *On The Line*, 1985, and *thewayofit*, 1988. These books may be 'little' in terms of their physical size but pack a big wallop. Like the phone box in Dr Who, they contain large vistas and spaces inside. These books exhibit both a fierce integrity of word placement, and a fierce cohesion. It is easy to be fooled by the fragmentary nature of the poems into missing the underlying unity of each book. In speaking of a poem from *On The Line* first published in the NZ Listener, Bill Manhire comments: 'the other pieces [In the book] supply it with a place where it can exist more naturally...*On The Line* is a short sequence where it is important to think of the relationship between poems as to consider the 'meanings' which each individual poem contains.'

I learned this the hard way when, originally thinking that this volume would be a 'selected works' I tried cutting out some of the poems I deemed to be of lesser value, I discovered that fierce cohesion. These poems have each other's backs. They proceed not only linearly, page by page, but as a whole create a verbal force field I couldn't mess with. In fact, there are *no* poems of lesser value, no dross here (although there are some I like better than others) and in each book the fragments compose a single entity. The precision that went into the shaping of each poem also went into the shaping of each of the 'little books.'

In the first book *upagainstit*, the layers of the world are peeled away to reveal a raw brutality:

the hills
whistle in

their
desolation

the core's
rock

histories'
bone

i'm meat
in the wind

There are no safeguards or comforting illusions in the world of *upagainstit*, a world of violence and pain, mostly expressed in the language of everyday speech, oral language, marked by an avoidance of abstractions and Latinate word forms. Sometimes the language is pasted directly from what someone has said, bits of found language, like this one coming from a gang member after the poet approached him about speeding up their little street.

see you later man
i'm just going to see

a guy
'bout his face

This is Rabbitt at his hardest, sharpest edge. No quarter asked for, none given. This is a world without redemption:

fear of fear of fear
goes on

a frenzied light
impenetrable

pure water
turns sour

Despite all this there is no despair or histrionic chest-beating. Far from it. At the core we find a stubborn stoicism, a rueful acknowledgment of what it feels like to be upagainstit.

        time produces
    a perpetual white sheet

In the next little book, *On The Line*, two years later, the same ruthless uncovering reveals something new – love. Love and a new playfulness. The book walks the line most elegantly, augmented by Jane Pountney's line drawings. It's a meditation on the nature of the line. It's not all sweetness and light, but it begins with the breath of creation, the line between existence and non-existence and moves on from there to discover the body as the body of love.

    a touch upon
    the arm

    an outstretched
    eye

    we have been
    here forever

    & today

The feeling of a blessing runs though these poems, along with an implied narrative, a love alluded to and left for the reader to imagine. This narrative continues in the third little book, *thewayofit*, 1988. The last book ups the ante in terms of this dive into love, which is now expressed in intimate tones, the hushed tones of pillow talk.

    watching
    trees sway
    softer

deep in
pleasure
& you saying

when was
it ever
better

to feel
your body's
shape

With regard to the role of Jane Pountney in the creation of the last two
little books, Lindsay commented in an email to me:

'You can't talk about *On The Line* or *thewayofit* without talking about
Jane. She actually put *On The Line* together, and featured largely in
thewayofit. As well as her drawings, done in a matter of seconds, poems
such as 'leave with me' and 'over land' were influenced by her charcoal
works. She was reading writers such as the French philosopher Julia
Kristeva, and ideas of language being a patriarchal construct, with
women speaking in the cracks of language. I'm indebted to Jane, she
taught me a lot.'

When we make the thirty-year jump to *Prayers for the Living & the
Dead*, we land in another narrative, this one covering the years of the
poet's life from age fifty-six to seventy-one, a period traced in forty-
seven pages of poetry. It feels like a big 'little book.' The method of
composition, the construction of minimalist blocks of language
remains the same, but the focus has shifted from the problematic 'self'
to the wider world, and Lindsay's family in particular. The first poem
after a brief prelude ('Let us remember our dead'), called 'day of the
dead' touches, in three short verses, on the poet's barber grandfather
('Keep your skull still'), his publican father ('Next, who's next') and his

own dead son ('Remember, remember me.') That first poem sets the theme for the bulk of the book in which the poet pays tribute to his various tipuna. The images are conjoined with an hallucinatory clarity:

It's dark on the Old Man,
dark on the Old Woman too:
the apricot trees are bare,

soon they'll pick the grapes,
a black horse appears
through the paddock gates.

The last dozen or so poems leave the immediate family and move to the wider culture of the poet's time and place in history. Poems like 'Needlework' evoke and celebrate the working class, the world of ordinary people, stoical and forbearing people who do things to get by and help each other. It harks back to the depression era of the 1930s. In the poem 'Everyday Christ,' which appears to be about William Blake, he evokes the 'everyday Christ' of the title, as 'hidden in plain sight.'
And once more, reported speech. The sounds of the human voice:

People are people
There's the struggle

I never wanted
To live this long

To become
An old imbecile

These are poems informed by clarity, compassion and tenderness. New (written since 2021) and Uncollected Poems we find the same method of composition, but with a further extension of subject matter as the poet uncovers more of the world around him. Here's brevity, humility and humour, a 'talking through/broken teeth.'

the sweet
wet earth smells
an earthy prayer

Lindsay Rabbitt's work with graphic images is divided into three sections. The first, *Set Piece*, grew directly from his interest in fonts from his typesetting days.

'I was working for Hutcheson Bowman & Stewart (printers) at the time, 1988. *Set Piece* was produced as a type catalogue. I hand-set the title and printed it on a letterpress hand proofing press.' (Lindsay Rabbitt in an email to me.)

These might be called concrete poems and showcase Lindsay's playfulness and humour; the idea of crediting fonts with a personality is inherently quirky and droll.

The second section, *Type-Cast*, continues the interest in fonts and the shape of letters extending it into blocks of bright colours. Image and word play with each other, and we're never far away from a pun. (On the subject of puns, Lindsay pointed out that 'a form (for locking type in) is also called a chase,' revealing a pun in my title quote.

In the 'Artist's Statement' that accompanied an exhibition of Type-Cast in the bookshop BAM (run by the late Neil Rowe) that once existed in the now-empty Wellington Public Library, Lindsay states: 'These screen prints are informed by my early training as a hand and machine typographer. From my understanding the word cliché comes from the French to mean 'cluster of type.''

'In the early days of movable type (single letters assembled individually to form a line of type) well-used phrases were pre-set to save time in a laborious task. Each generation reinscribes the meaning of some words. Words differ according to their placement and context. They are constantly being emptied and filled with meaning.

'Colour becomes coded and differs from country to country: flags, road signs, corporate identity, cultural use. It also works on the senses.'

Of the third section *Light & Shadow*, photographs, writer and photographer Martin Edmond says, 'Lindsay Rabbitt's photographs have the simplicity and the concision of his poems; as well as their mysterious resonance. They suggest that a plain view of the things of this world may yet disclose the strangeness of how and where we live; that depths become apparent only when you have learned to see surfaces. Like the visual poems in Type-Cast, these images are enigmas which, when deciphered, do not lose their enigmatic quality. Rather, their power is augmented.'

Lindsay's ongoing interest in photographs (he regularly posts them on his facebook page) began, in a hand's on way, when he worked as a newspaper reporter who had to learn to take his own photos.

Lindsay Rabbitt's work is austere and uncompromising, yet warm; empathetic yet wry; tough yet tender. They are intensely mediated, yet give the impression of spontaneity. They are firmly grounded in common vernacular, yet give the impression of philosophical depth and intimations of the spirit. In these poems you can feel language as a physical force, primal utterance, language as emergence. Their openness brings the reader in as a co-creator, sharer of the poet's discoveries, participants in the poems' enactments.

Enjoy.

Mike Johnson
Waiheke Island
February, 2024

upagainstit

letter from holloway road

the evenings are drawing out
movement is more pronounced

late sun makes an eye sparkle
a lip slips across foliage

currency is exchanged
at gateways

light wets tongues . . .
even the silent are articulate

street motion

you don't realise
the speed

> *ah no - you just*
> *go faster*

> *see ya later man*
> *i'm just goin' to see*

> *a guy*
> *'bout his face*

it was so close . . .
fear, an ambiguous

colour, flashed
an image

of a different
hue

gorgonised

the hills
whistle in

their
desolation . . .

the core's
rock

histories'
bone

i'm meat
in the wind . . .

memory's
a rock

that looks
like a head

you couldn't
miss

on the way
to Dunedin

in 1950s London
Uncle Gordon

spotted Big Jim Erica
from our hometown

he appeared
Gordon said

like a familiar rock
on the Knobbies

upagainstit

my face is
there in the mirror

looks as if
i don't belong to it

looks at me looks

looks as if
it wants approval

i read
strangers' faces

framed
by a window

not yet
broken

there must be
somewhere in the middle

to see both sides
of that mess

instead of being
in the middle

of this one

green somehow
makes up the day

water sparkles
on its lip

a kid kicks
a can of dreams

as a kid i used
to ask God
to come see me

now i would be
quite happy
to go see Him

nothing's surer

night & day's
peopled
the patter
leaves marks

pagan eyes

he's skinning
the hawk's head

    flew into
    a train

    fractured
    its skull

& he's digging
its brain out . . .

cleaning the fragile
bone with a knife . . .

    goin to make
    an icon

    to grace
    the horror

nevermore

Gauguin painted
a Tahitian beauty
with a raven
& what seems
like conspiring
neighbours

Gauguin had just
been treated for
the clap

a Hockney pool

i surface from
the dive

looking for
the splash

the pool-side is wet
bodies bake

i feel the belated
sting of impact

i swim thru
the water

shadows nibble
my heels

an expanse
of sky

holds nothing
but itself

my wet flesh
attracts a breeze

a cloud rolls
across a revelation

i make eyes
at the sun

me as art

it's my ambition to paint
not only to paint

but to paint myself painting
as if to image vanity

in such an overt way
as to nullify it

what's left to say

you say you neither belong
to the cloistered or the worldly

& suicide seems a solution
what's left to say to that

(take up embroidery or tennis?)

i nod sympathetically
saying i know, i know,

try being dishonest

hermit

i've no need
fur people

them with their
strangeways

justme
anme animals

till i go
to ground

shadow

from where you are
a shaft of speckled

light enhances mystique
i am scared to move

it's said

the word is shadow
shade is to play around

form
for Alan Loney

so many times
i seem to be back

naked, weaving a cloak
with no pattern to speak of

vanity demands a tapestry
need requires a covering

time produces
a perpetual white sheet

black earth

with a need for order
in the clustered regions

with a need to have
precise sight

i set about
to weed

the garden

till all i see
is black earth

the crunch

i've no need
to go that far

i've no means
i mean by all means

flesh wants flesh
wants flesh

flesh flesh wants
flesh flesh flesh

w-a-n-t-s

f-l-e-s-h

shit scared

fear of fear of fear
goes on

a frenzied light
impenetrable

pure water
turns sour

how did we do

here hiding now
a kid shouts

a scrambled
language

hear the next
dull thud

against a
roughcast wall

all the time
a music plays

how did we do
hell, it's not finished yet

icon

i've no need
for it

it just looks
right

the way
the light

hits
its head

ON THE LINE
with drawings by Jane Pountney

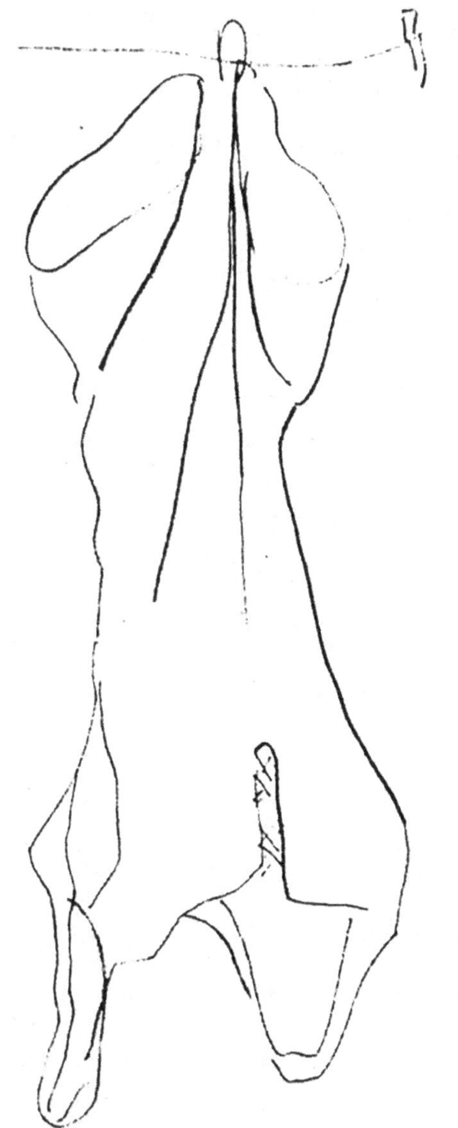

the line
is the lie

the world
is . . .

the world
is flat/

allofasudden
a tree stands

up straight

white stretch
of land
print in
the mark
leave depleted

a night of
banging doors
& receding heels

a day
recording
the echo

turn on the light
& you have
your own shadow

turn to the light
& you have
silence fall

on one shape
after another

i'm not up
to it

struggling
against the line

leaving my marks
everywhere

still
still here

as quiet
as breath
the hills breathe

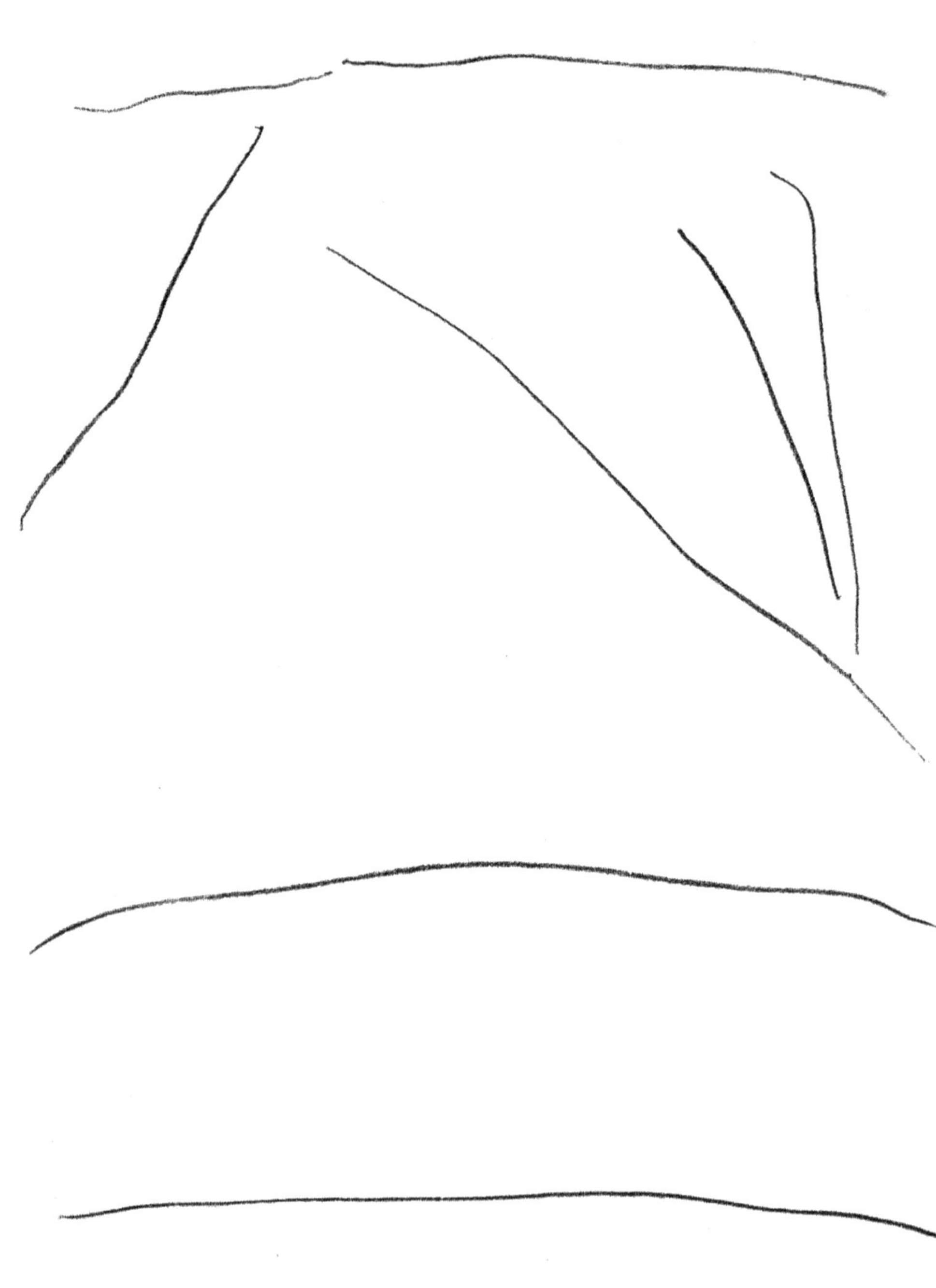

form of flesh
and line

histories
contortion

coming closer
to consciousness

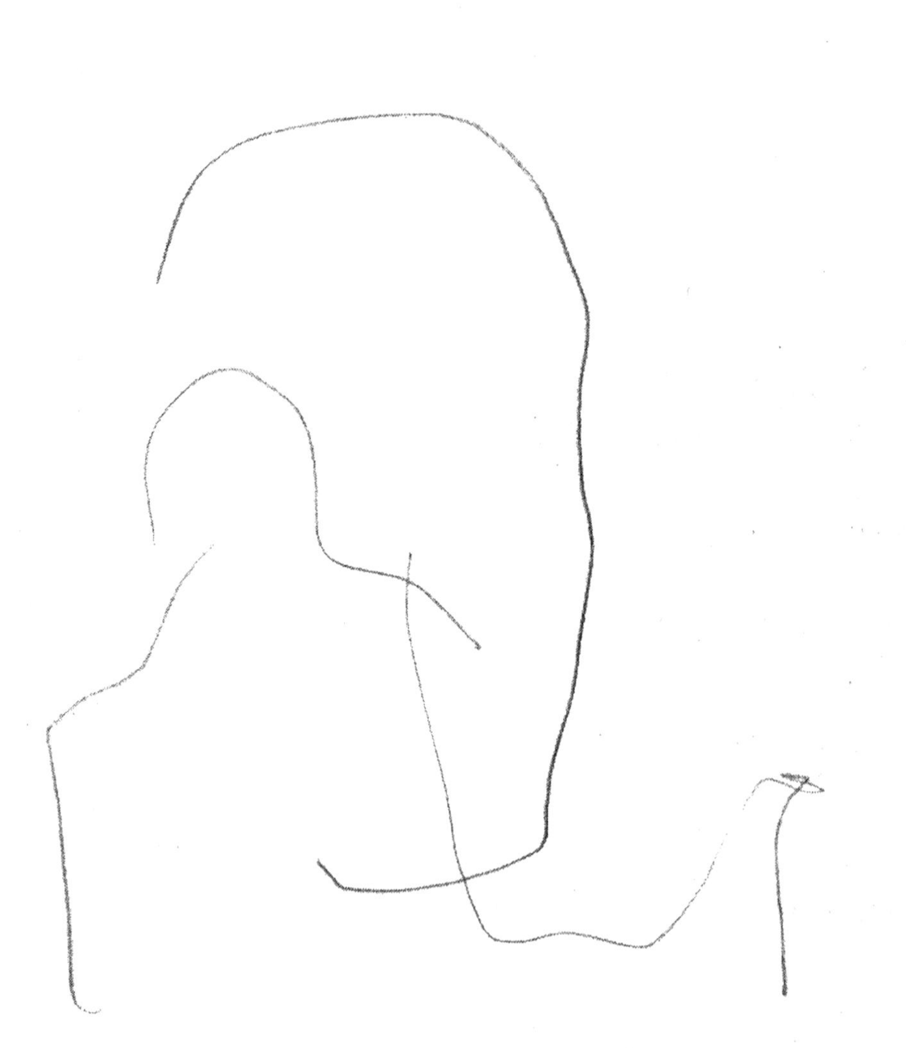

peopled
        this space

of soft corners
& open doors

a touch upon
the arm

an outstretched
eye

we have been
here forever

& today

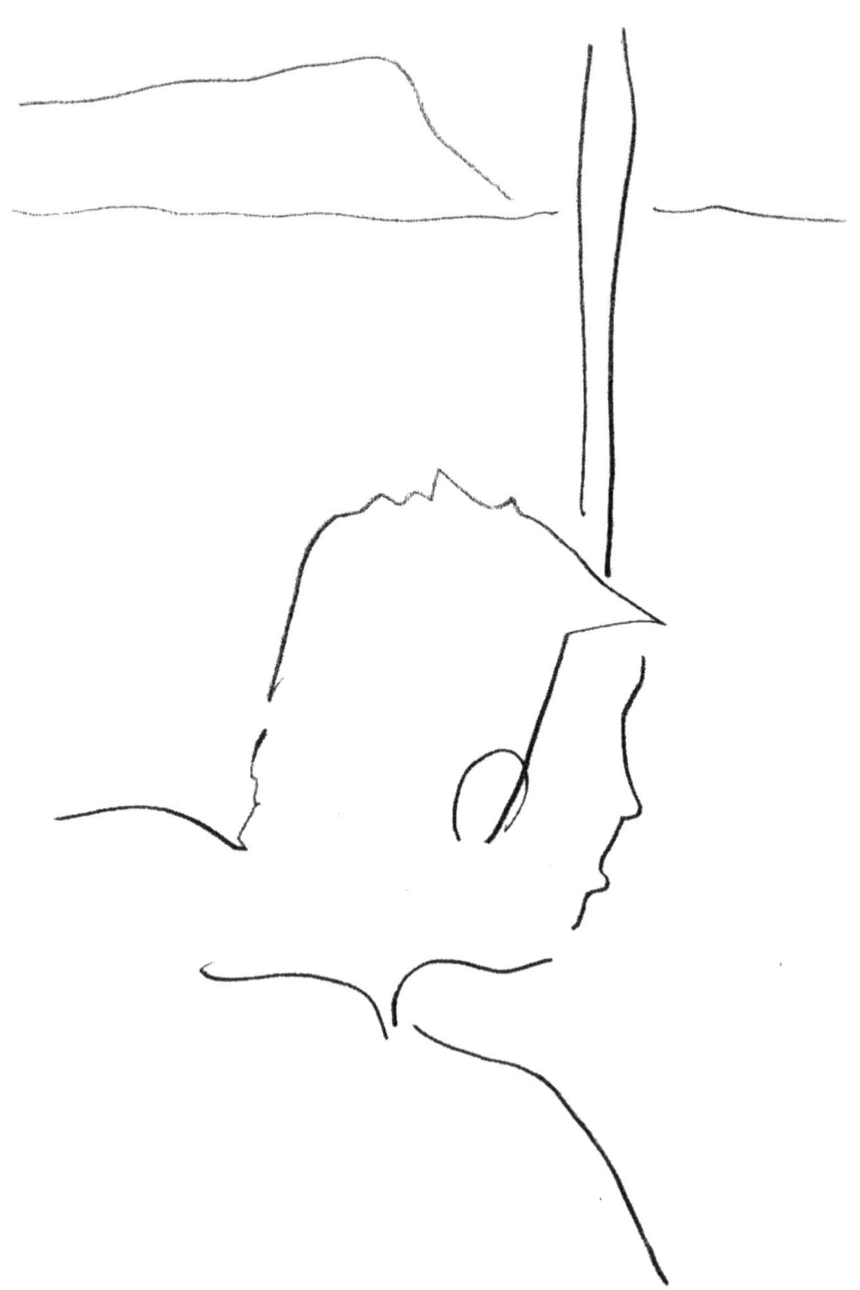

mind now
the way home

catch cold
with indifference
of air

take the crackle
out of your anger

take care
of yourself

lift
the weight
out of your body

light up
there

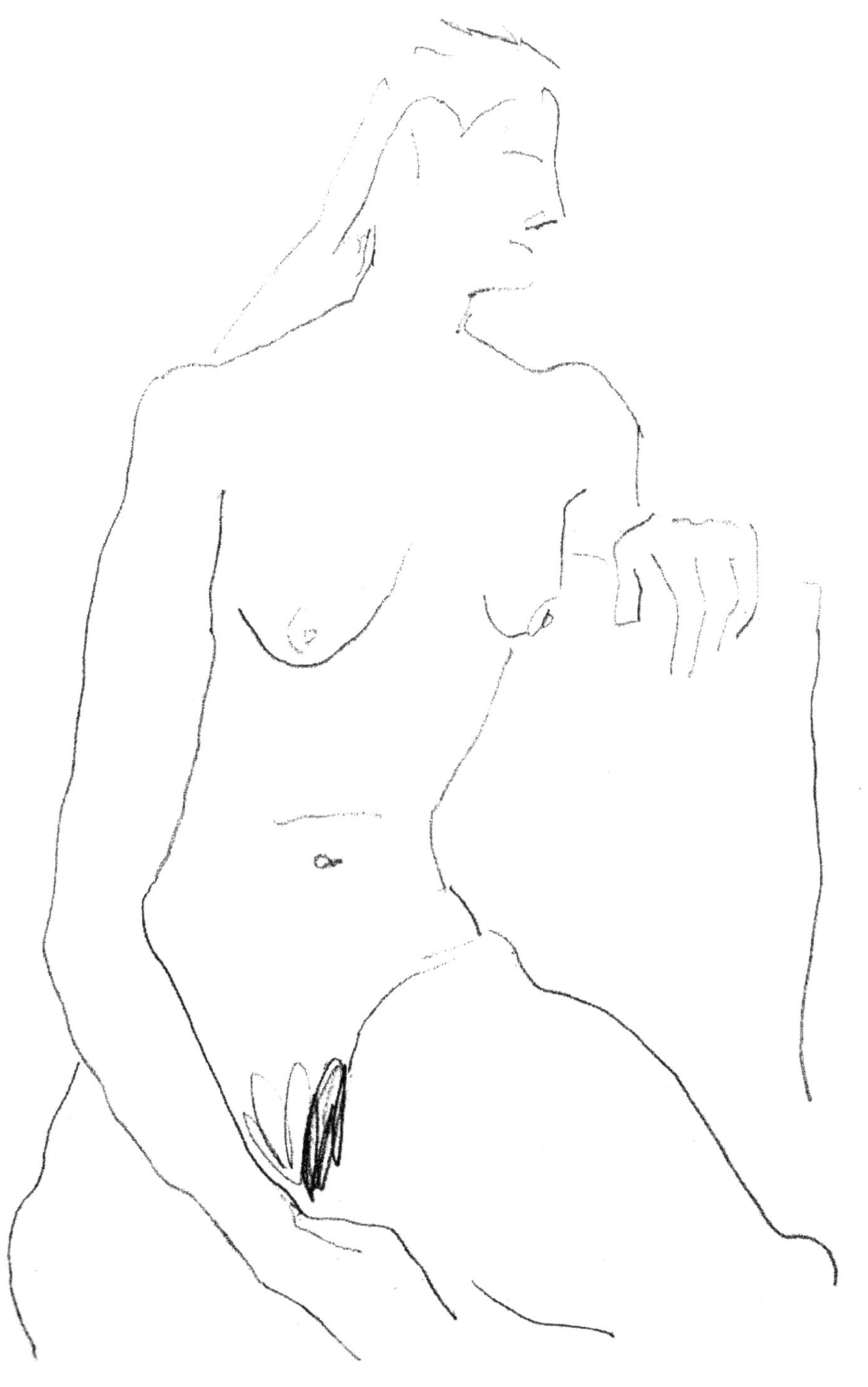

it's not a matter
of physics

think of sex

soft pit
of ancestry

think of you

sun
in your body

sun
on your face

sun
on that hill

music sounds
across the valley

at last it's hot
the sun, i mean

without wind
a white butterfly

feels space
everyone is

taking off
their clothes

a bee does
a perfect loop

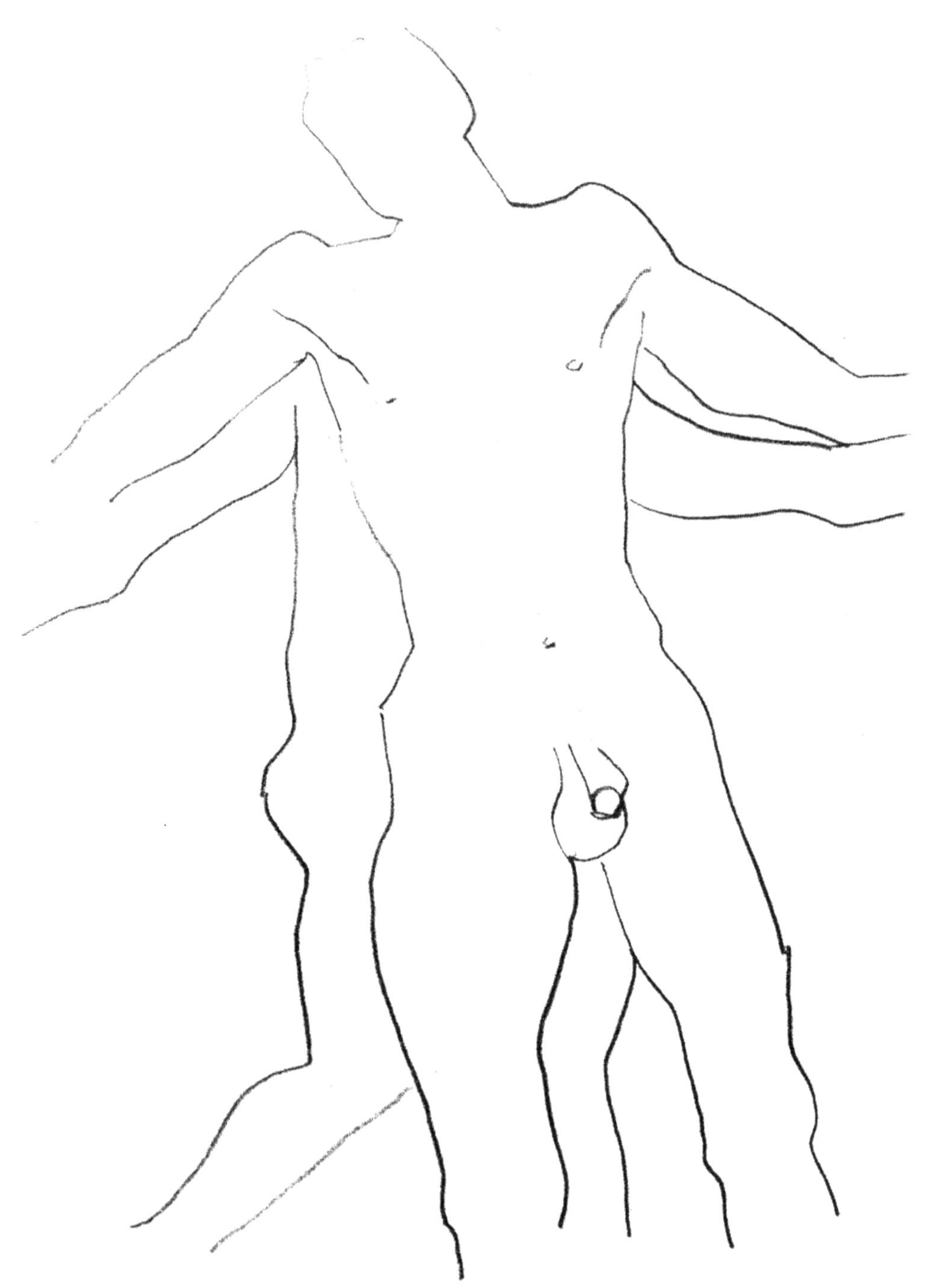

the music's
on the tongue

the feeling's
in the body

dance
to the rhythm

watch yourself turn
do it again

move on
forever

it's you

that inhabits
my content

outside there's
a fine rain

a touch of hurt
a heave of fear

swelling toward
the throat - tell me

how the hell
did this happen

was it when
i told you

just one time
too many

that i loved
you - was it?

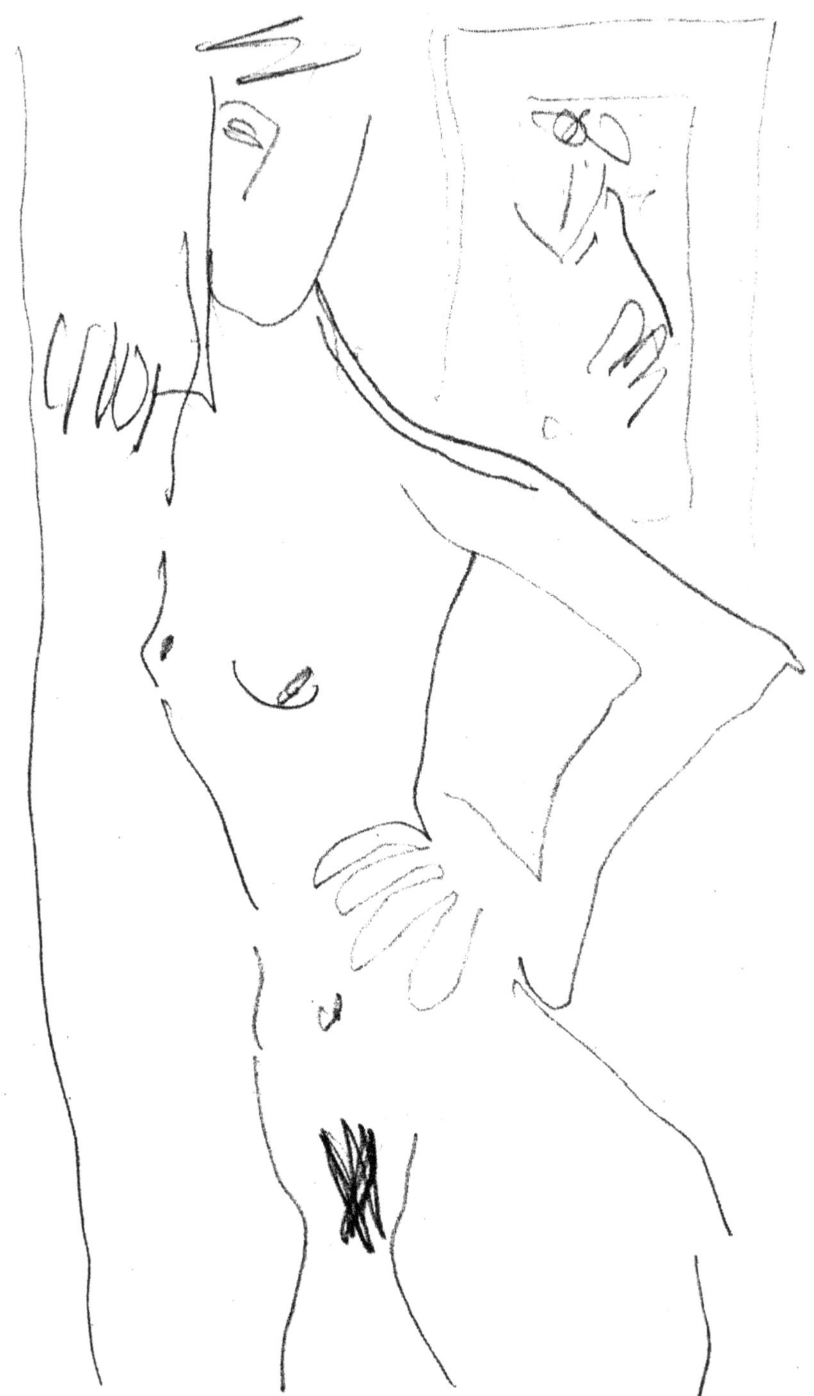

that line
is getting
a bit wet

too slippery
on the tongue
to mean anything

in your spare room
the line's been drawn

the hue's filling in
could be skin - could be sun

colouring in
an arc then a circle

remember back
to the old place

an assortment of self
a scatter of animals

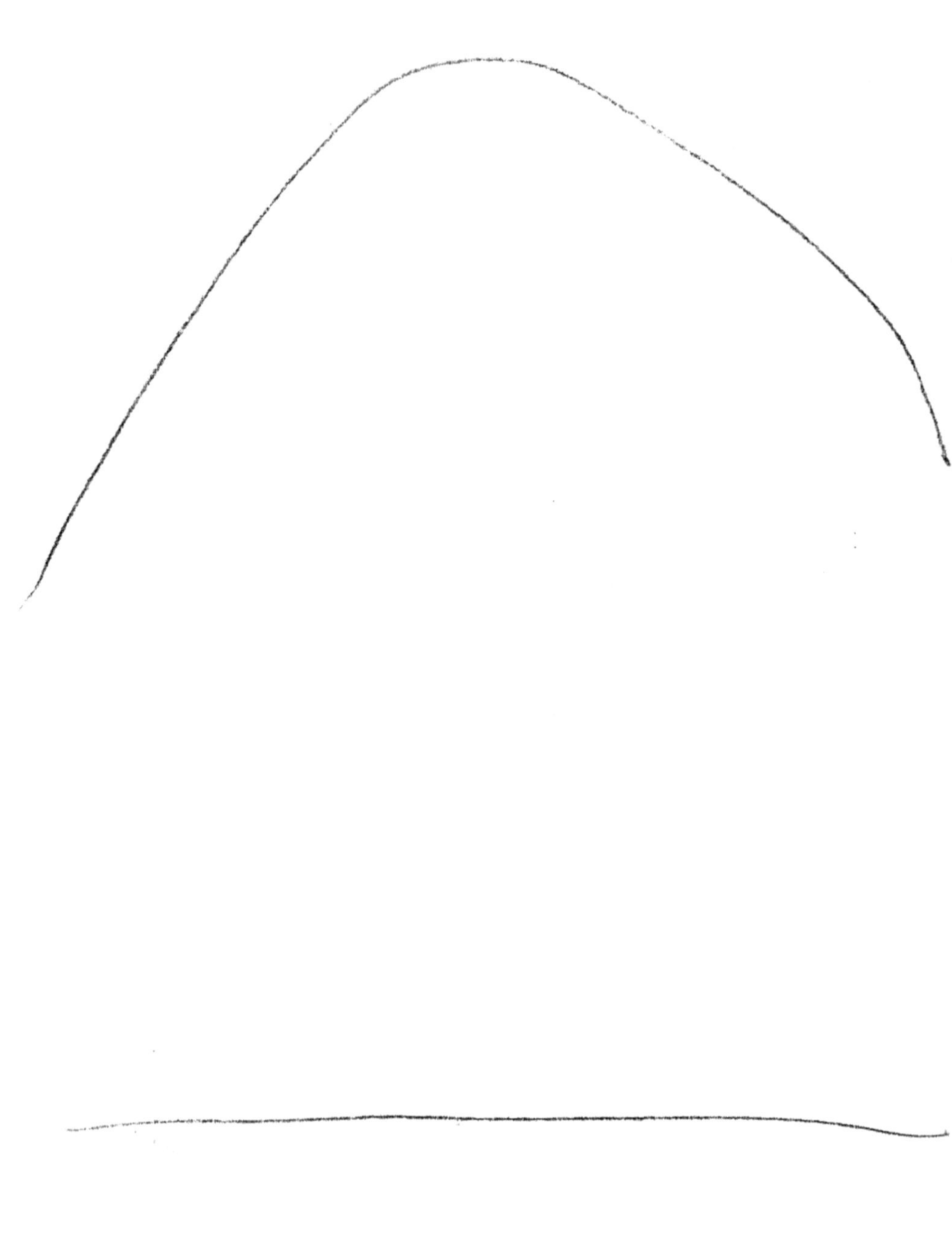

it's too big
for us

to handle
leave it

where
it is

thewayofit

with drawings by Jane Pountney

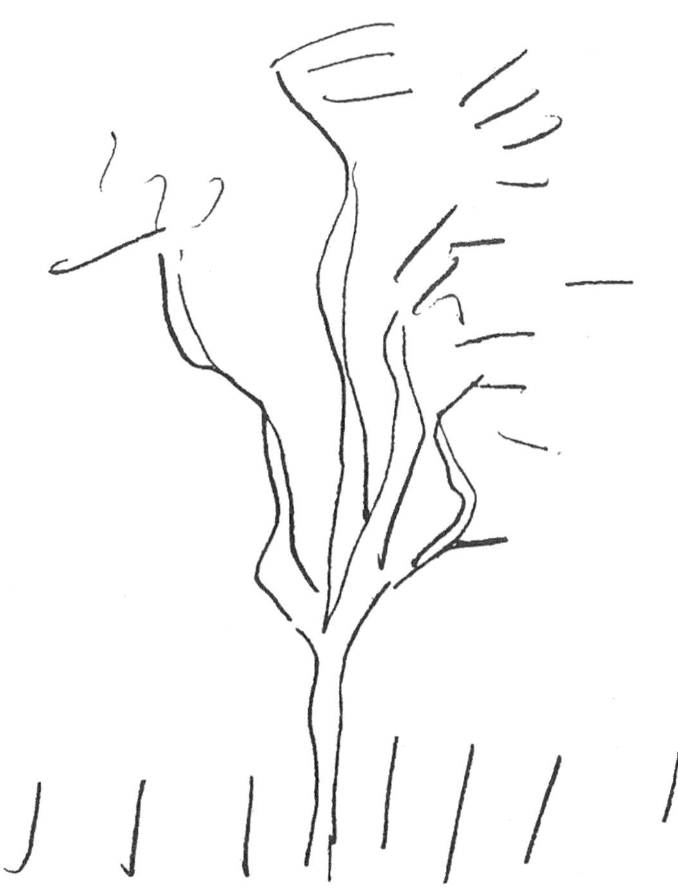

opening up

the sea holds
jumping silver

light
a gull

lands near
then opens up

to the blue
drift

foreplay

enter

the voice
the eyes

of a woman
setting you

at ease

taking in
the light

dances
in your eye

music

hear
your heart

beat

no time
like the present

thewayofit

dream of

the animal
richness

of sex
figurements

smooth
rub

invent

a language
for

the fine
features

of morning

listen

voices
rhythm to rhythm

expressing
an easy affection

he catches
his breath

as she opens
her mouth

the sky's
prime time

the sun's
tongue

face facts

the earth
secretes

& so do we

to make much
of the act

when you
thinkofit

it's a
rollercoaster

blue
or is it red

we came
to understand
simple works
just well

you draw
the curtain

O

a floating
moon

your face
half-lit

then open

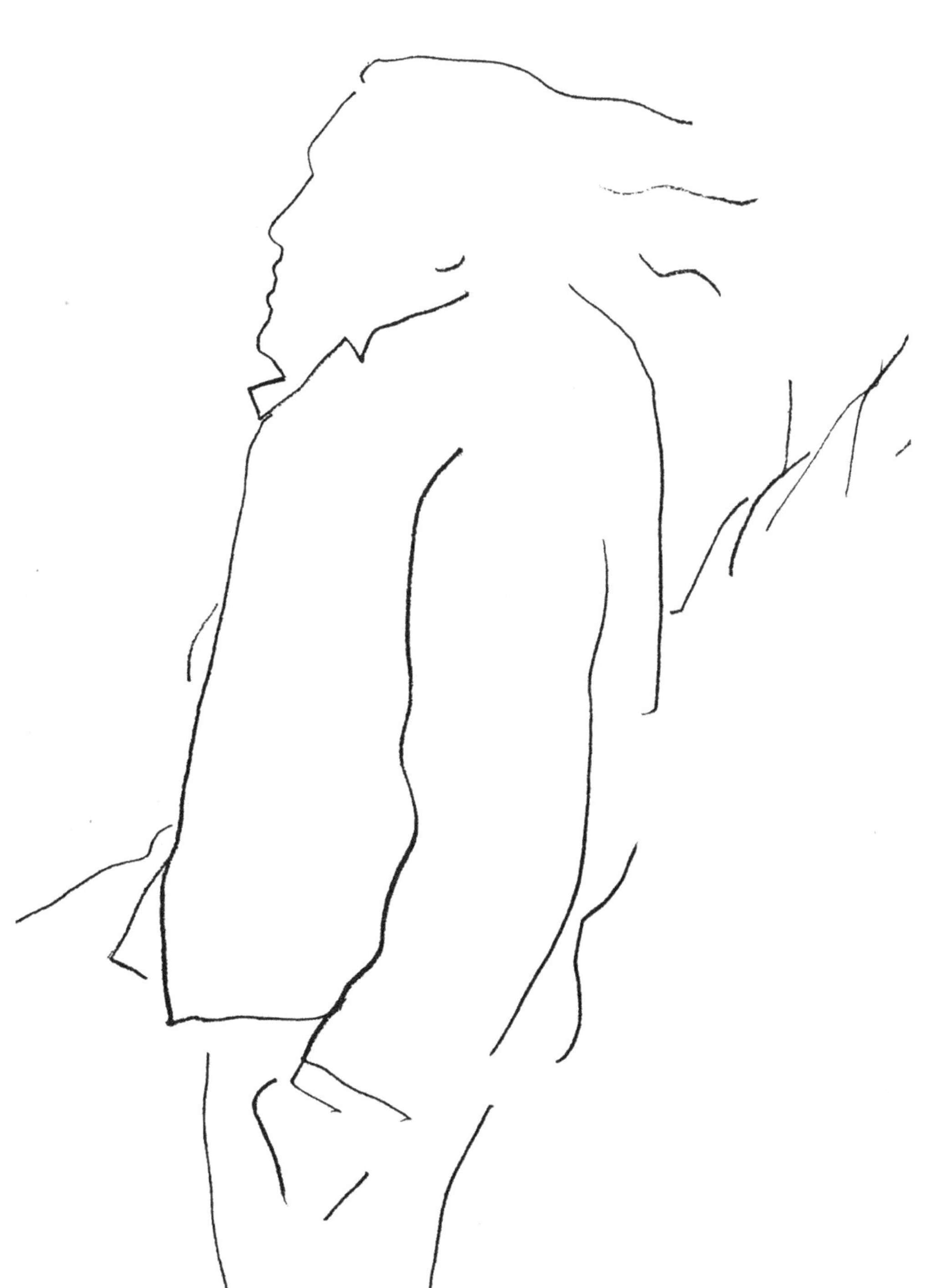

riddles

i dig up
light

shine
the present
thing

a lovely bright
clarity

they climb
over themselves
reaching for another

over land

you think
the land-
scape

you huddle
in body
wrap

you stride
out of
yourself

you think
in chest
heaves

you talk
in a language
you don't understand

elements
marvelled

ground
questioned

rising
to the length

& breadth
of bodies

delicate
acknowledgments

desire

to live by it
the half-
remembered

washed by
sleep you hold
the image

you are inland
but it is the sea
it's more than water

influence

fluent
weather

facing all
of us

process

you
now enter
i

two
single
pronouns

finding
each
other

shadowed

now you turn in
your thoughts

alone you
case the visual

i stand in the shade
of an old tree

lightness

watching

trees sway

softer

deep in

pleasure

& you saying

when was

it ever

better

to feel

your body's

shape

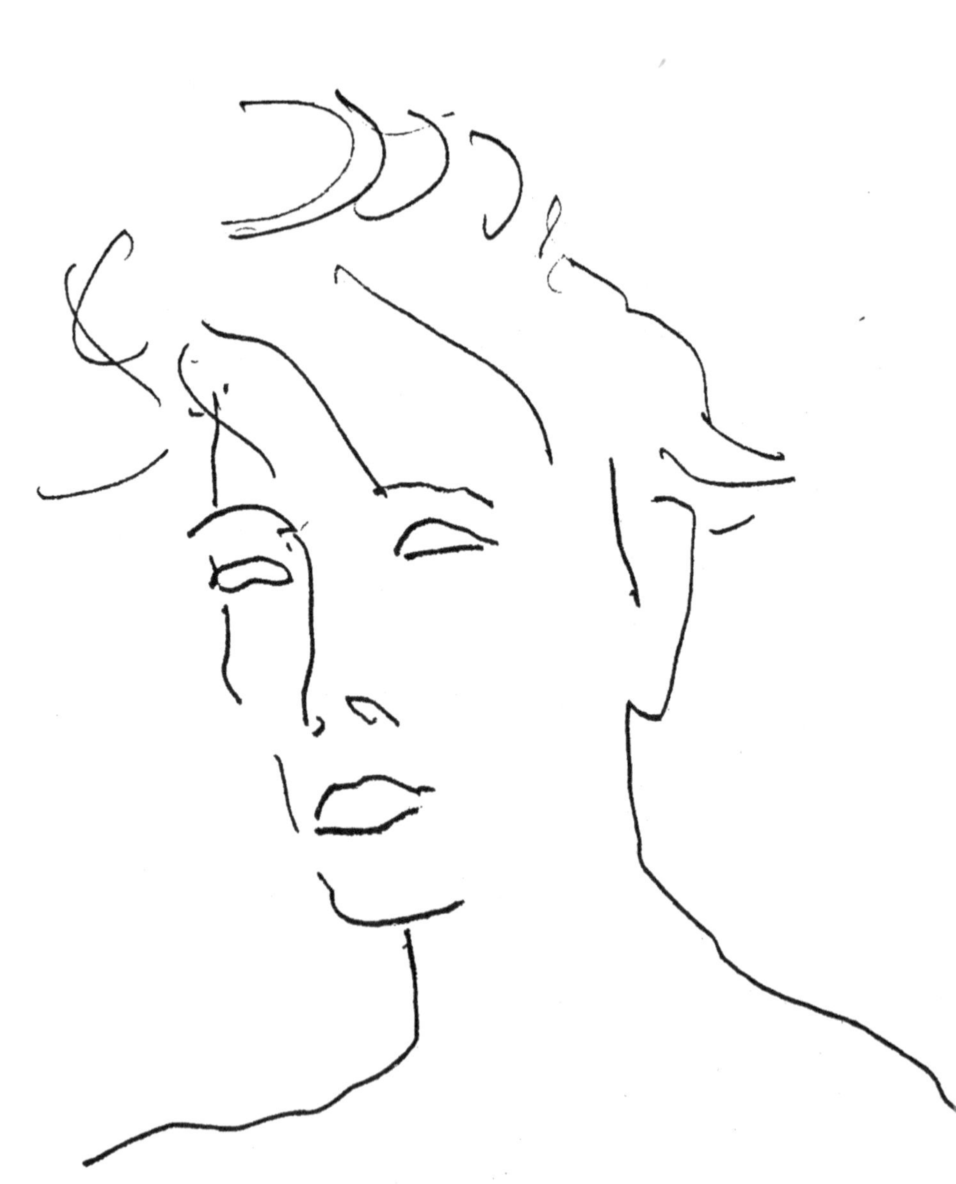

leave with me

the black
& white
of it

shifting
the occasional
shadow

each day
getting
older

in effect
i am myself

just like you

who else
could we be

remembering
a site

we create
another

to our own
liking

one body
two body
three body

every body
going back
& forward

over land
on water
in space

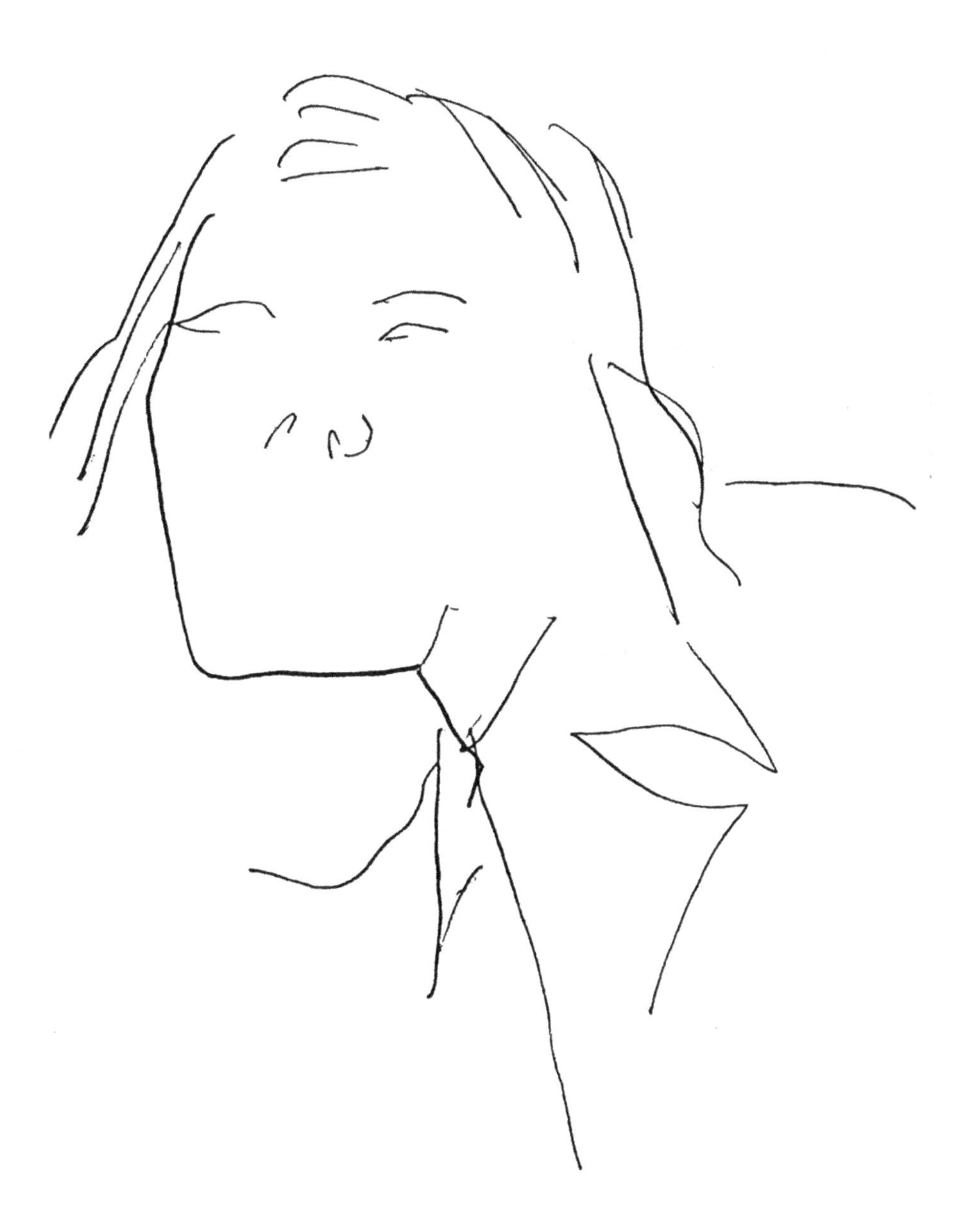

shifting points

look see
here it is

what's
to happen

now that's
forgotten

a gain

memory
origin
of thought

scratch
of a broom
on a concrete path

take back
all you
taught me

& the
instant of
your departure

do not say
now you're
all alone

for i
remember
many things

we had
in common
not to be

brushed
aside
as slights

of desire
or in deed
that which fed

the mind's
machinery
flashing emotions

of daily
content filled
with light

out-of-sorts

searching
for balance

he tipped
the scales

at his own
weight

the problem
was a psychological

one & all
were in agreement

finding
a measure

he became
old stock

the kids

here
they go

busting out
to live

barely touching
the ground

heads every-
where

street
talks

side
walks

look right

take hold
the edge

is
the centre

you know

you wanta be
out there

where it's
happening

moving
like some

slick machine

with eyes
like that

anything
could happen

don't interact
just lookout

caught in the gaze

inland water
lies between
you & i

the island's
clouds roll
. . . bruised

dogs bark
at every
sound

you turn
to see more
than you think

the awkward
swaggers you
catch yourself

living in
this not so
perfect place

take heart
take to the soles
of your feet

a way

a line
on the
face of it

evening
light
after rain

politics
of the
mind's arc

SET PIECE

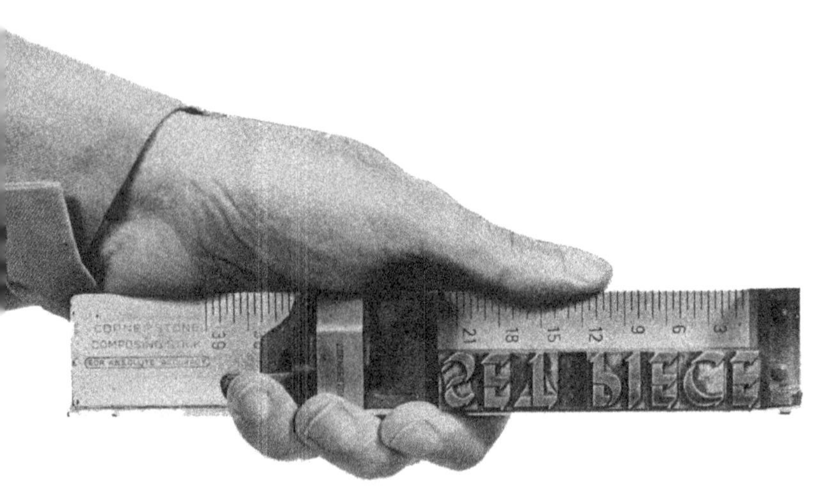

CORNERSTONE
COMPOSING STICK
FOR ABSOLUTE

PALATINO & PI Font

i'm dead in the
hand of ☆s

waking
i ☆tle myself

the body eclipses
i to 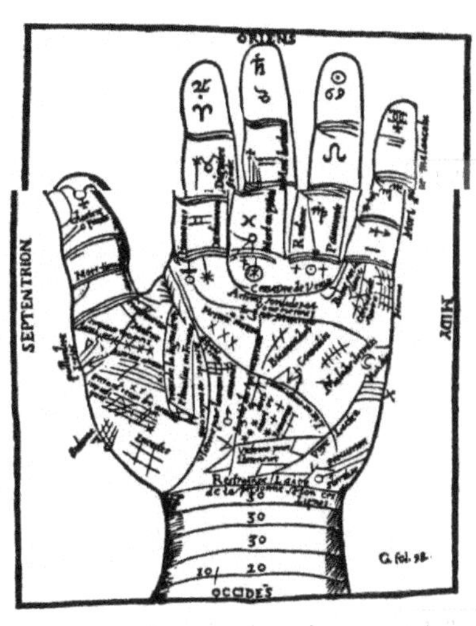

dark to light
justlikethat

i bark
one sharp syllable

SABON

can we lift ourselves
with the syllables

TIMES

The political ones are ***eating***
They have their *mouths* full
Their *eyes* dart over
The paper wars they are ***creating***

L U B A L I N

ZAPF
he
saves
on every-
thing leaving
room for a few more

Type-Cast

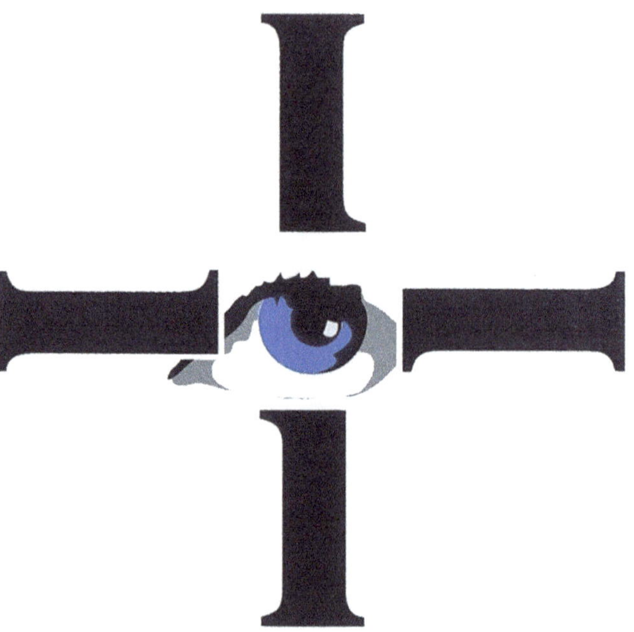

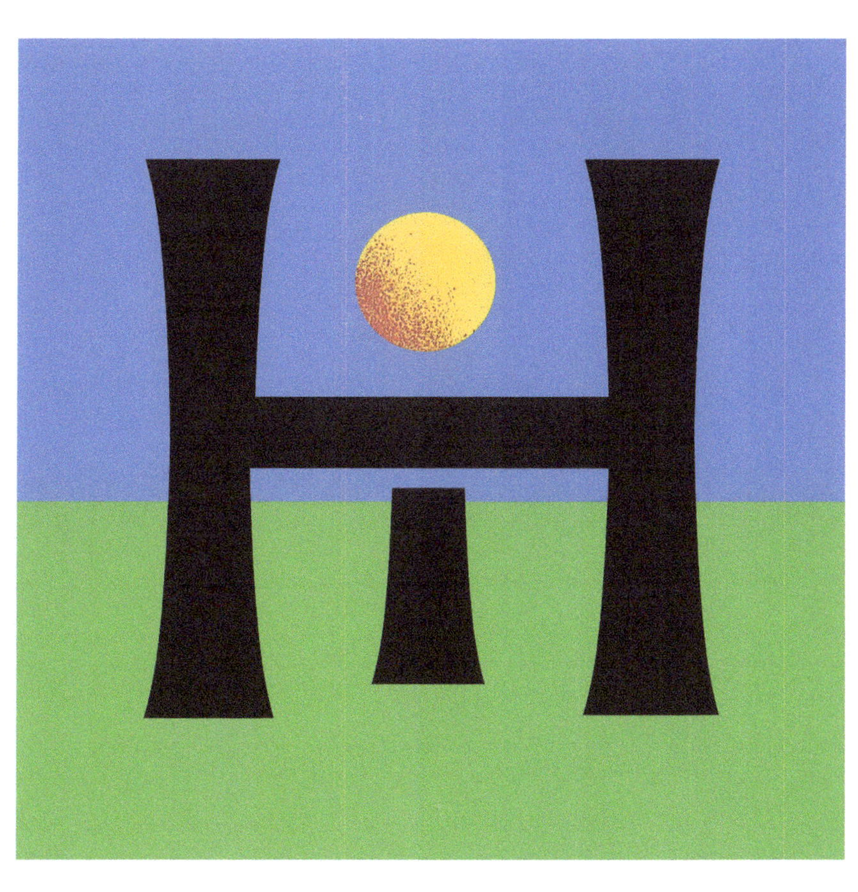

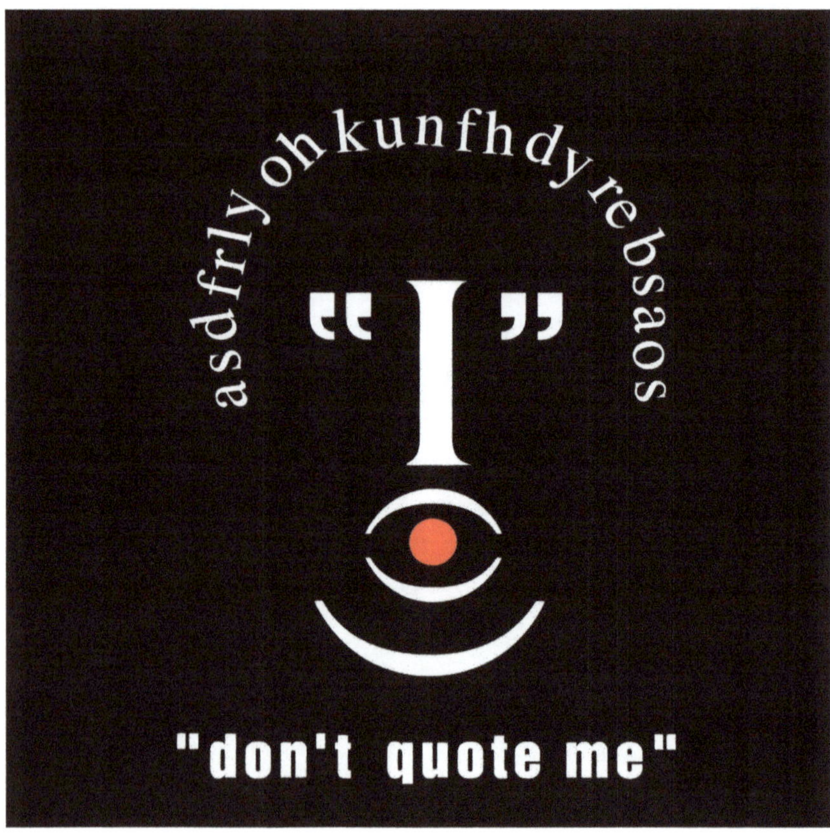
asd frly oh kunfhdy rebsaos
"I"
"don't quote me"

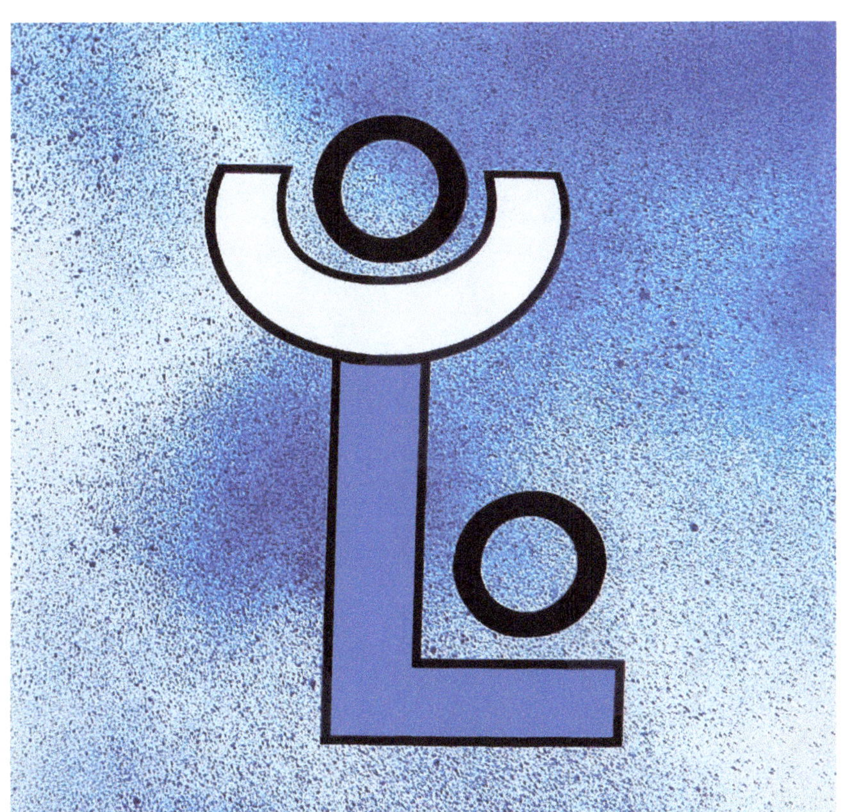

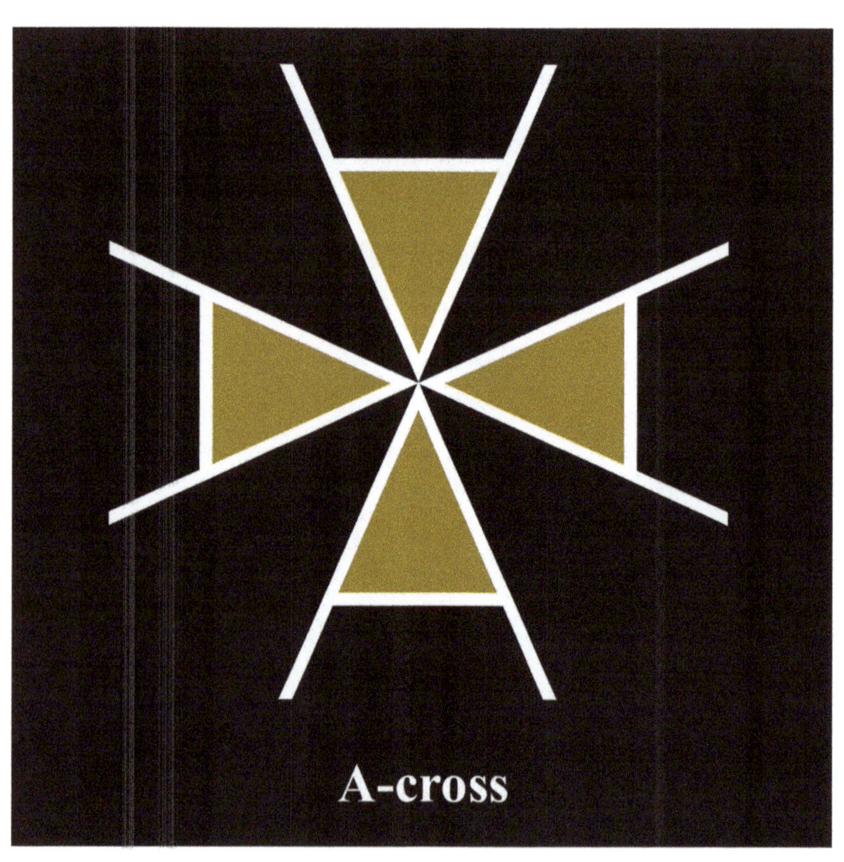

A-cross

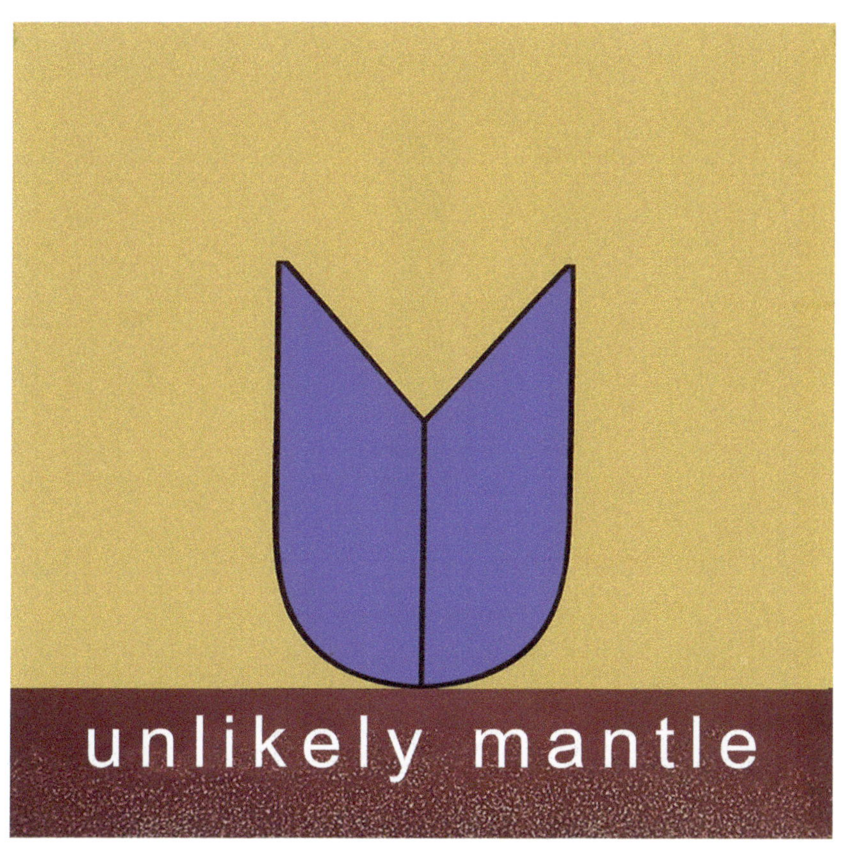

unlikely mantle

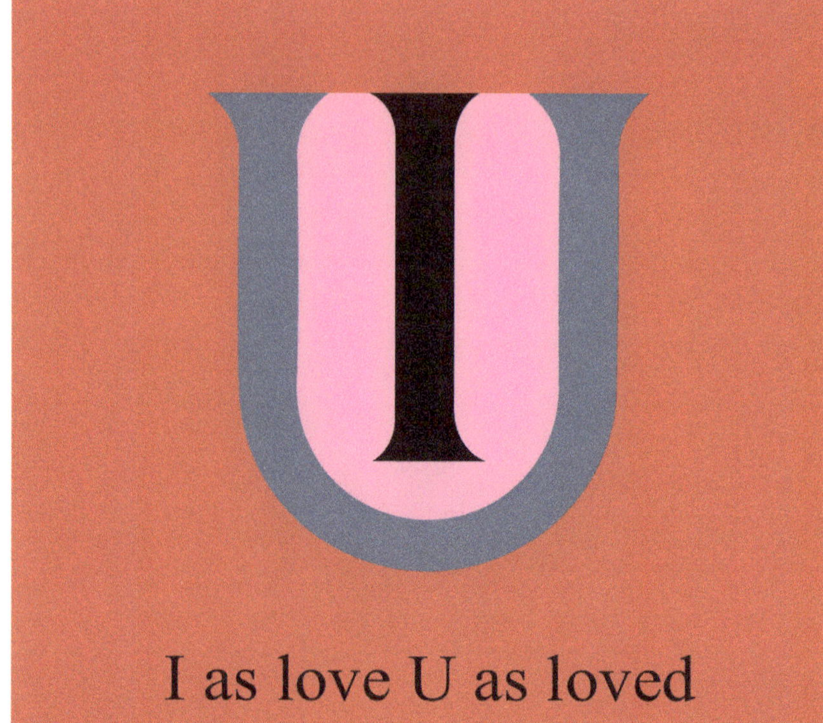
I as love U as loved

bait

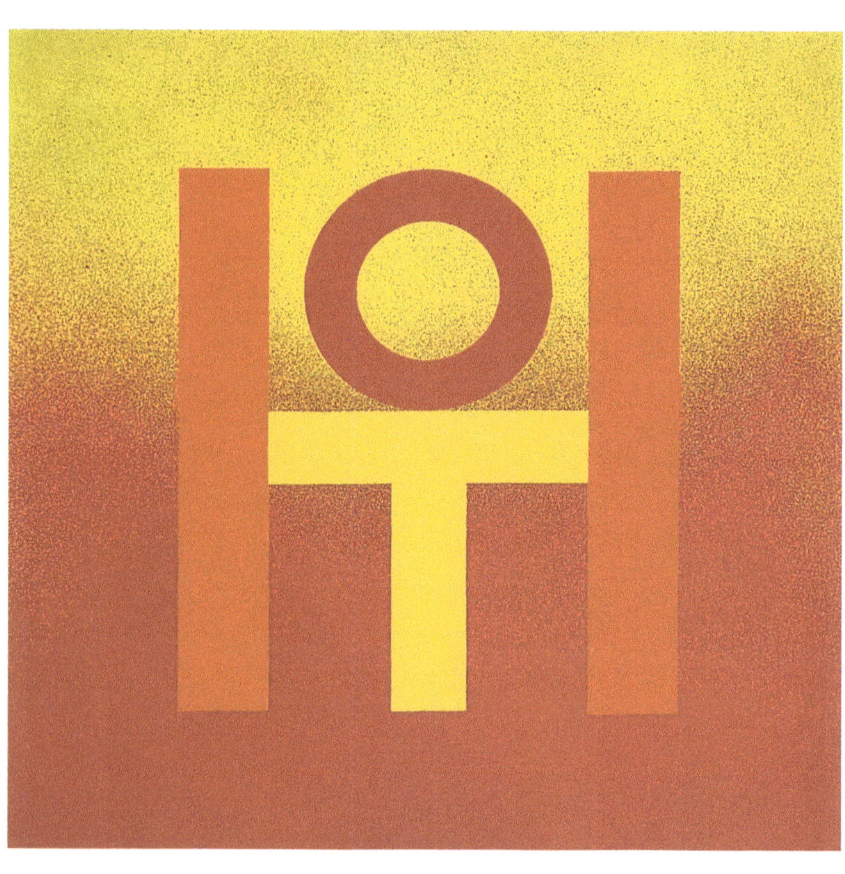

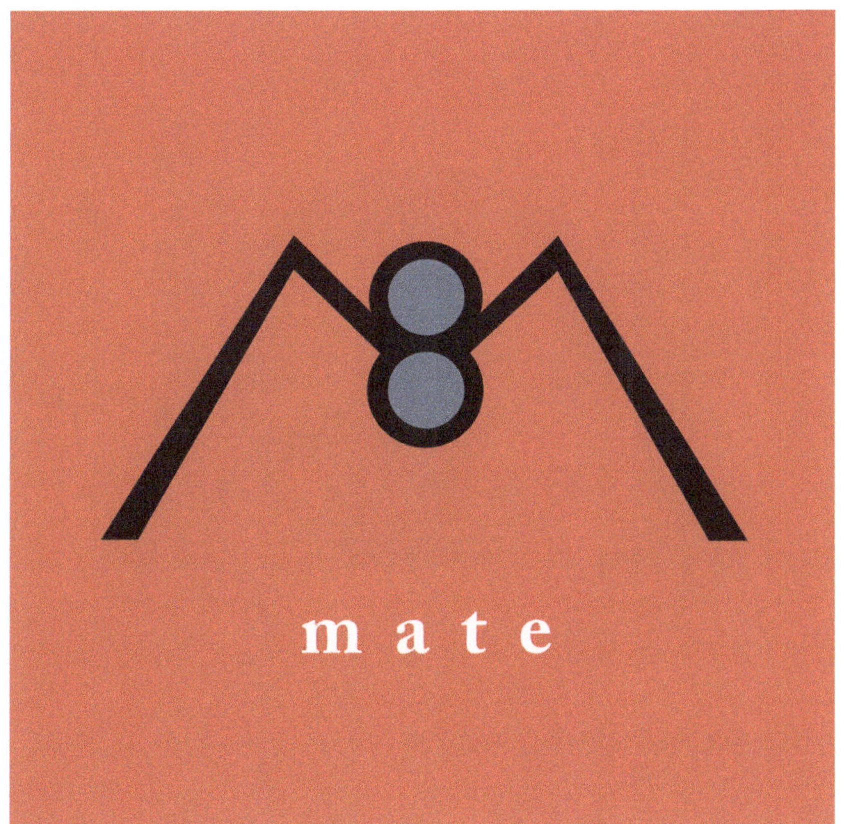
mate

a question within a full point

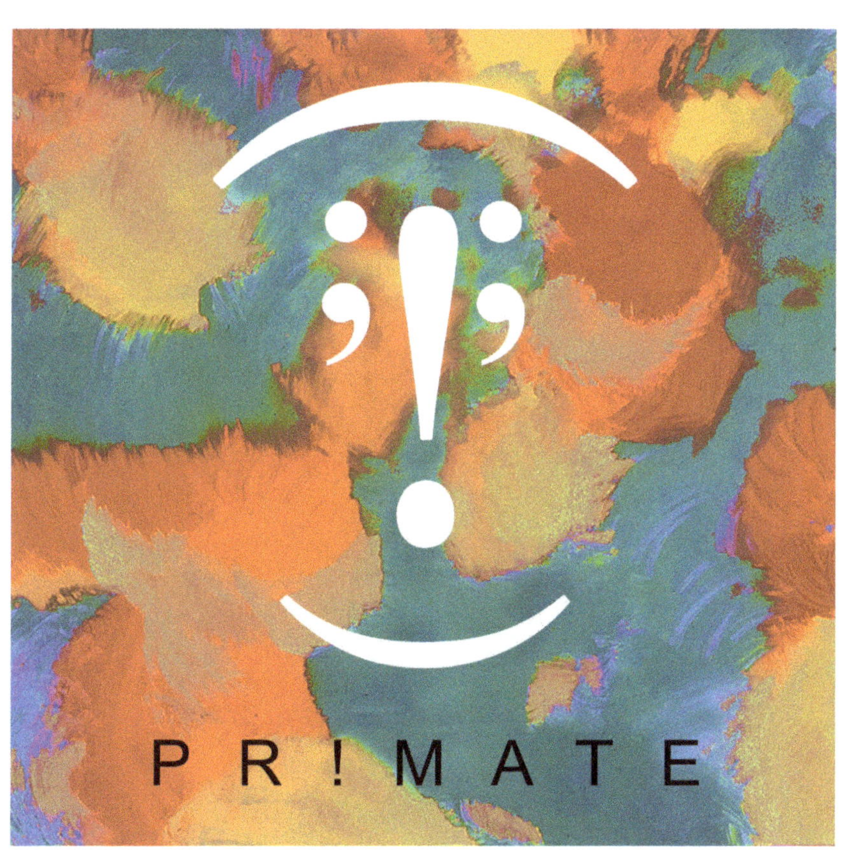
PR!MATE

Prayers
for the Living
& the Dead

with drawings by Bodhi Vincent

PARADE

Let us remember our dead
on this morn singing with life.
Let us bring out our lovely dead -
where there's beauty, sorrow will follow.

DAY OF THE DEAD

My barber grandfather,
dead for 23 years,
whispers in my ear:
'Keep your skull still.'

My publican father,
dead for 19 years,
chants above the din:
'Next! Who's next?'

My sweet son,
dead for 7 years,
smiles as if, as if to say:
'Remember, remember me.'

- November 2, 2007

THE BEATS

Allen Ginsberg wept when he heard A Hard Rain. He wept
for Bob Dylan's blue-eyed boy. He wept for joy. He wept

for William Blake. He wept for Walt Whitman. He wept
for the freewheelers Cassady and Kerouac. He wept

for the Cosmic Corpse inside his American head.
'Chant from skull to heart to ass,' he said.

At Phill's place The New Millennium Beats
beat and strum. Beat and strum, illuminated

by two dollar candles. Raumati, 2006, is a world
away from New York, 1964. But the spirit flies

a warped course. Twelve-year-old Isaac plays
his Sonic drums like the guy in The Grateful Dead.

I dig it. My heart thumps in the ribcage
of an ancient man. My mind is a foetus

in the womb of a black woman. I walk home
under a descending moon. The sea is milky.

The village surreally lit. The stars bleep & blip.
Our drummer boy sleeps like an angel.

WALK TO DAY'S END

The day starts out chilly blue
& drifts into gunmetal grey.
When I reach The Esplanade
the sea's a briney soup
of kelp & seaweed.

Low cloud obscures
Mana Island & Kapiti
is a hint of herself.
I button my coat
up to the neck.

I, a man of 59,
going nowhere
in particular,
just walking,
mind talking,

& lo & behold
on a breakwater rock
a juvenile fur seal.
We trade curiosity
for uncertainty

& the wee animal
slips from rock
to sea, swims a while,
turns, dark global eyes
speak vulnerability.

I double back, round
the corner, up the hill
to my two-room shack,
where I tidy up,
take an afternoon nap,

wake to the radio,
time pips counting
down to the news,
'Michael Jackson
has died aged 50.'

So the day ends in a prayer
for 'the man in the mirror',
the moonwalking pop star
who couldn't sleep.
O Michael rest in peace.

BROKEN ANGEL

Evening prayers
Morning rounds

Rolling gurneys
Urgent sounds

Who's to die
Who's to say

Who's to take
The fear away

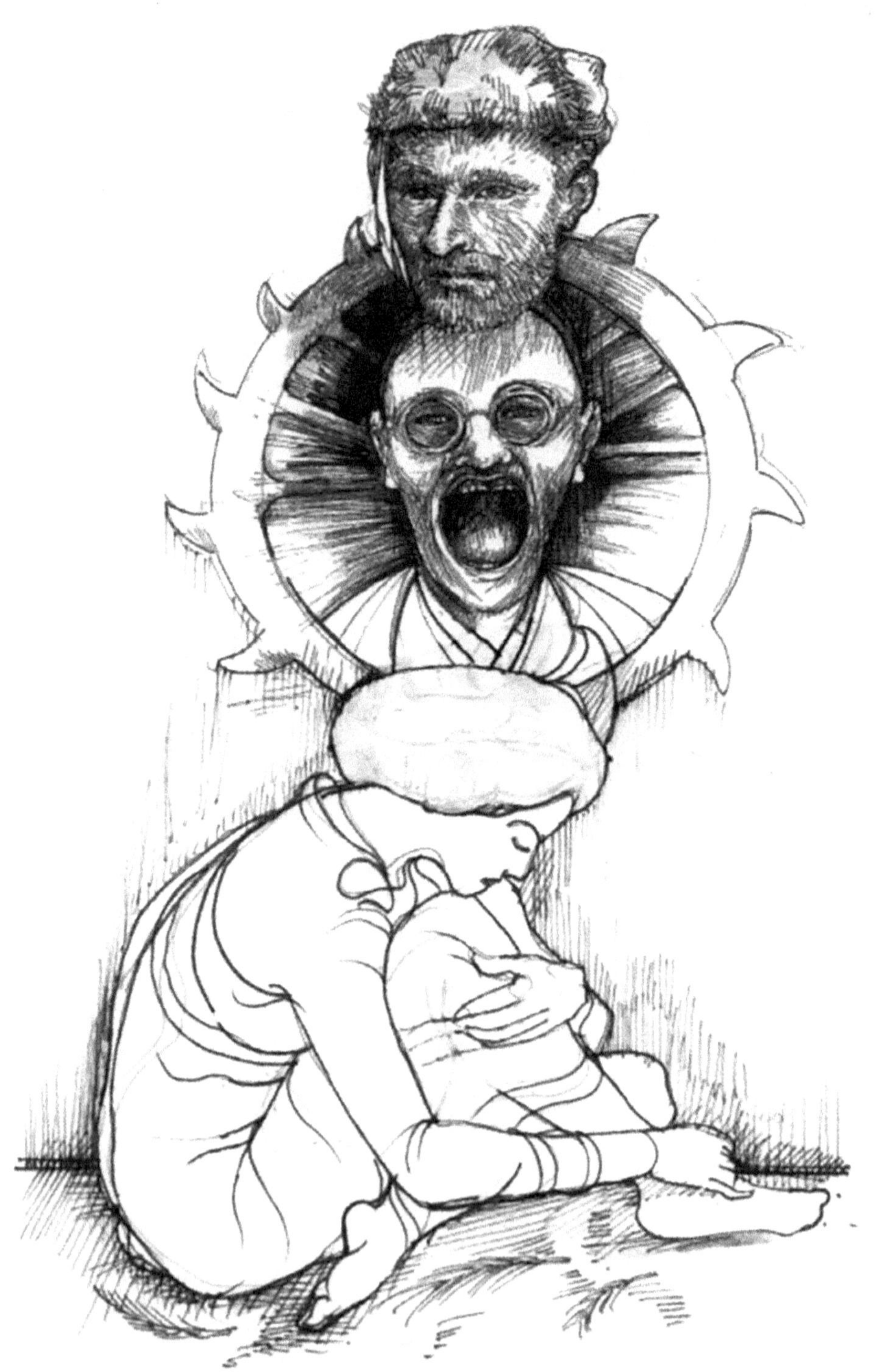

PICTURES

the track back
the track ahead
the carts carrying
the recent dead

the Screaming Popes
the horse's head
buried in
Jack Woltz's bed

a waking scream
a curdling scream
another spin
on a Catherine wheel

in Julian Schnabel's
At Eternity's Gate
Willem Dafoe as
Vincent Van Gogh

for Paul Gauguin
cuts off his ear
but hands it to
a hooker instead

a waking scream
a curdling scream
another spin
on a Catherine wheel

& Mads Mikkelsen as
The Priest sees ugly
in Vincent's
essay of beauty

created in ecstasy
by a painter of light
who contrastingly suffers
from horrible fright

a waking scream
a curdling scream
another spin
on a Catherine wheel

the track back
the track ahead
the carts carrying
the recent dead

VILLAGE LIFE

Morning's a procession
of pram-pushing mothers;

feathery rain
and that blackbird again

on the same branch
in the oak tree;

a mongrel dog, ears pricked,
exercising its happiness gene.

Evening's dinner and tele-
vision - a komodo dragon

dismembering a goose
on Komodo Island;

a dream of wind-blown
white cherry blossom

& Mick's suicide,
a muted drum, an empty swing.

APOCALYPTIC

Top ape, nigh on 8 billion of us
to poke & prod the wilderness.

She protests in hissy fits,
spits sparks from fiery pits

& sets to work sleety cold,
whirling, whirling from the poles.

The gadgets have seized,
cleverness is deceit;

what was is null-&-void,
solar flares put paid to that;

the poles have reversed,
the sun revolves around the earth.

BREVITY

People are people
There's the struggle

I never wanted
To live this long

To become
An old imbecile

Exaggerated
Self diagnosis

She delivers
Pitch perfect

People are people
There's the struggle

THE WALLANDERS

Find someone
to sit with you,

you're not strong
enough to sit alone,

says the artist father
to his policeman son.

Tangled
with Alzheimer's,

he paints the same
sparse woodland,

sometimes with a grouse
in the foreground.

NANO SLEEPS

P's told the same story
six times in an hour.
She nods off, then
her snoring wakes her.
'I'm going to write a book,'
she says, 'Will you edit it?'

P lives with M,
her 40-year-old son.
He was institutionalised
for 2 decades.
Schizophrenia was diagnosed.
He learnt the art of silence.

I read him the road code
for half an hour each week.
I ask him questions to test
whether he's taking it in.
'What's the two second rule?'
He furrows his brow.

P jolts awake. 'Did I tell you
I'm going to write a book?' she asks
'It's inside my head,' she says.
I'm taken by her open mouth,
by the shape it makes
when she sleeps.

ALL OR NOTHING

I wake with a bastard hangover;
the night's detritus weeps and crusts.

I contemplate death/pure living,
joining an order not yet found.

I go to Lorca for comfort. Alas,
all he gives me is a thrashing sea

in which I cannot drown.

O POOR MAN

Outside it's warm,
inside your house is cold;
your heart is cold,
your liver cantankerous.

You've been mean
with the furnishings,
you've been mean
with yourself.

O poor man,
O poor, miserable man,
it's no fun to visit
your house of discontent.

UNFURL

Walking the yard
Spitting out mandarin pips

Looking at the lanky
Becoming unruly broad beans

Eyeballing the cauliflower
Broccoli hybrid

Which is near-to-being
Harvested. Yes, you mostly

Reap what you sow
This ageing body

This mind minding
Its own unknowing

RAUMATI SUNDOWN

The coast follows
A cartographer's curve

A colony of swimmers
Stands waist-deep

And the sun melts
Into history

That's the point
You see

A place to hang
Your ancestral hat

After all we have
To belong somewhere

PRAYER FOR LEON

'Every atom belonging to me
as good belongs to you . . .'

As good belongs to you, Leon.
We pledged at Boggy's and Emily's

prayer will wrap you at sundown.
This evening I sit mellow

as mist sits on the hills
reading Whitman's Song of Myself:

'I loafe & invite my Soul.'
The deep green trees sway

to a cosmic bass line.
The beautiful sky's singing, Leon:

Every atom belonging to me
as good belongs to you.

HELEN 1962 - 2012

I'm relieved you've been spared embalming:
You look like yourself, just elsewhere –
your energy dispersed around your house,
whispering in the trees, in the air.

I recall the young woman who suited her grey hair,
whose smile radiated the length of Dale Road,
who hailed me down to say, 'Hello, I'm Helen'.
It must have been 1997, & we became friends.

Friends & fellow travellers, fellow strugglers,
who'd talk about their troubles, the redemptive
nature of art, how life is a day-by-day proposition.
See you Helen, in the night sky, in the wild beyond.

MAYA

Maya, born in London to a Japanese
mother & an Antipodean father,
is today's smoking companion

outside at Lembas Café. She talks,
you listen. Her discourse covers
Shintoism, ancestor worship,

the humble nature of the everyday
Japanese, who, she says, religiously
save for weddings & funerals.

DANNY

Danny, the Welsh chef,
ever so carefully lattices
his prawn terrine
with zucchini strips.

His attention to detail
is palpable, loving . . .
'Like,' he says, 'putting
a baby to bed.'

DELIVERY

Shy boy
in the
doorway

handing
over his
light touch

MEASLES

She's on her haunches
in the passage-

way over a child's potty,
her face flushed red.

He's shooing his son back to bed;
there's anxiety in his voice,

the kid's ill at ease.
Previously he'd measles,

which, he's told later,
he'd passed on to his mother

& that the measles
had caused the miscarriage.

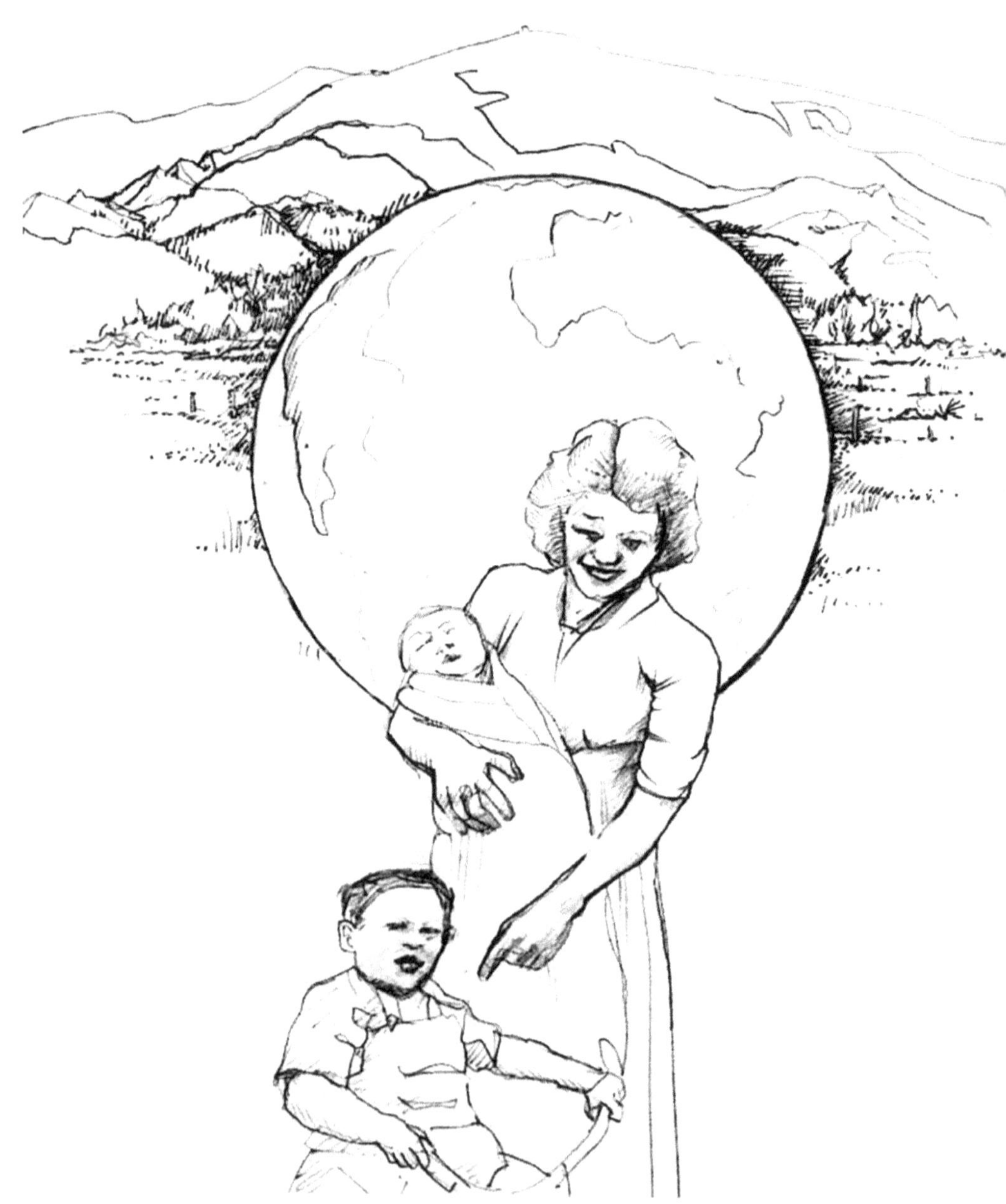

THE 1950s

The 1950s
Shang-eyed my life
Sunburn to echo
Pings under the ice

Bounceback
The Hydrogen Bomb
Behind closed doors
The Cold War

Sunfrocks &
Flagon beer
A dog's nose
A clip on the ear

The 1950s turned
On a sixpence
For the pictures
& an ice cream

It disappears
Then comes into view
Hey your mother's
Calling for you

I was a child
Of those days
When Doris sang
& Winifred played

FLOWERS

This pink evening is birthed from a blue day.
The old woman gardens with the aid of a walker.
Her husband looks out the kitchen window,
'She'll be sore & tired,' he mutters,
'in no fit state to cook dinner.'

My mother suffers;
but gardening makes her happy.

For my 63rd birthday she sends flowers.

BETWEEN WORLDS

You fantasise about leaving
all that is familiar;
letting go the corporeal

which in reality is a calling
heard by the other worldly
who travel holy space,

or felt by the unredeemed
driven into oblivion, or
sensed by the old ice people

who walked into whiteness
& died, you imagine, dreaming
of the day they were born.

After seven days rolled
over in the underworld
at the mercy of a deep sickness

you come to this recovery
room grateful, relieved
to be alive, almost well,

& yes, you'll settle
for almost, as it's long since
mother counted your toes

& fingers, little digits turned
spindly, almost translucent
in the blue afternoon light.

It's dark on the Old Man,
dark on the Old Woman too:
the apricot trees are bare,

soon they'll pick the grapes,
a black horse appears
through the paddock gates.

It's dark on the Old Man,
dark on the Old Woman too:
hawk circles, swoops out of view.

Is it feasting on rabbit or road kill?
Has mother given birth
to a boy or a girl?

POST & TELEGRAPH GIRL

Joy's sixteen, uniformed -
grey slacks & jacket,
blue shirt & black cap.
She rides a Raleigh bike.

Mrs Robinson greets her,
reads the cablese, exclaims
with joy, 'My boy's
coming home next week!'

She takes Joy by the hand
& girl & woman dance
up the hallway to the kitchen
where they have a sherry drink.

'I was just a girl,' Joy says,
'a little tipsy in my uniform,
riding back to the Post Office,
toward the end of the war.'

NEEDLEWORK

Before she married,
Hazel Ernestine
tailored men's suits,
tatted lace for dresses;

then she sewed
her children's clothes,
made ends meet
during The Depression.

As an older woman,
she crocheted blankets
knitted jumpers for
her children's offspring;

she'd talk about her father,
her mother's tapestry
of a childhood home
stitched from memory.

DAD

Dad had lovely hands,
they flowed as he spoke;
he danced a kind of jig
when he told a joke.

Dad was an outgoing man,
fast with a witty quip:
'Make a noise like a two-bob
piece & I'll come quick.'

Dad ran a good pub,
his punters an earthy mix;
in the Maniototo,
on the road to the Styx.

Dad served the thirsty
who worked this arid land,
& gladly took their money
with either lovely hand.

MAY

In the Southern Hemisphere
May is the saddest month,
But sadness is no bad thing.

I was born in May,
My father & Uncle Bryan
Died in May:

Their last breaths and my first
Placed in autumnal time
When the big oak shed its leaves
And my grandfather raked them

Into piles. In May we make
A pact with death. We make
Our wills. We stoically tend
Our part of the world.

CATHOLIC TASTES

I heard it on the radio: Kennedy's death; the assassination attempt
    on Pope John Paul; Alistair Cooke's Letter from America,
    his stolen bones; The Rolling Stones; Dylan Thomas's
    A Child's Christmas In Wales.

I heard it: the Wahine disaster; the standoff in The Bay of Pigs;
    the Boxing Day tsunami; Lee Hatherly's sexier-than-sex
    voice; Vera Lynn singing there'll be bluebirds over
    the white cliffs of Dover . . .

They washed over me – the voices that repeat, repeat. The voice
    that recalls Peter Snell's Wanganui mile introduces
    a Burt Bacharach tune. Listen: Leonard Cohen's singing
    the Sisters of Mercy . . .

Ours was a Pye – valve, cased in bakelite. Now I have a Groupmen
    clock radio – digital, slipped in plastic. Ah, an amalgam
    of memories! I wept, admittedly drunk, listening to Pita
    Sharple's maiden speech: Tihei mauri ora! Kia ora.

Ah, ock aye! Oh, me, me, my, my . . . Neil Young stays forever
    in 1969, & Tom Waits croaks: It's time, it's time, time, time,
    time . . . In the Helen Young studio Dave Dobbyn sings
    his Welcome Home . . . Haere mai, haere mai . . .

Oh, the chant that pulls a crowd! I drift, dance with the stars –
    step out of a Norm Hewitt interview: What does it mean to
    be a good man? It's common sense, he says, & I paraphrase,
    Love the wife & kids, & go easy on the sauce.

LOOK

The river
Boat . . .

A body
On its tender

A wash
In its wake

The body's
For a pyre

The body's
For a burning

For a burning
On a pyre

Being built
On a bank

Being built
In the moonlight

In the middle
Of the day

WILD CHILD

You come to this point
spun with doing words:
shower, shave, dress, eat,
wash up, walk into the yard . . .

In a concrete crack,
self-seeded & beautiful,
a dandelion, reminiscent
of a sixties' wild child.

BOB

Love poems
have a way of sounding
like Robert Creeley.

Dig his one eye –
His iris of dead reckoning.
His flower of truth.

MENACE

They're lovely guys
when not being monsters.

Rush the trigger-happy chap.
Run from the bloke with the knife.

O man, from making love
to the taking of a life.

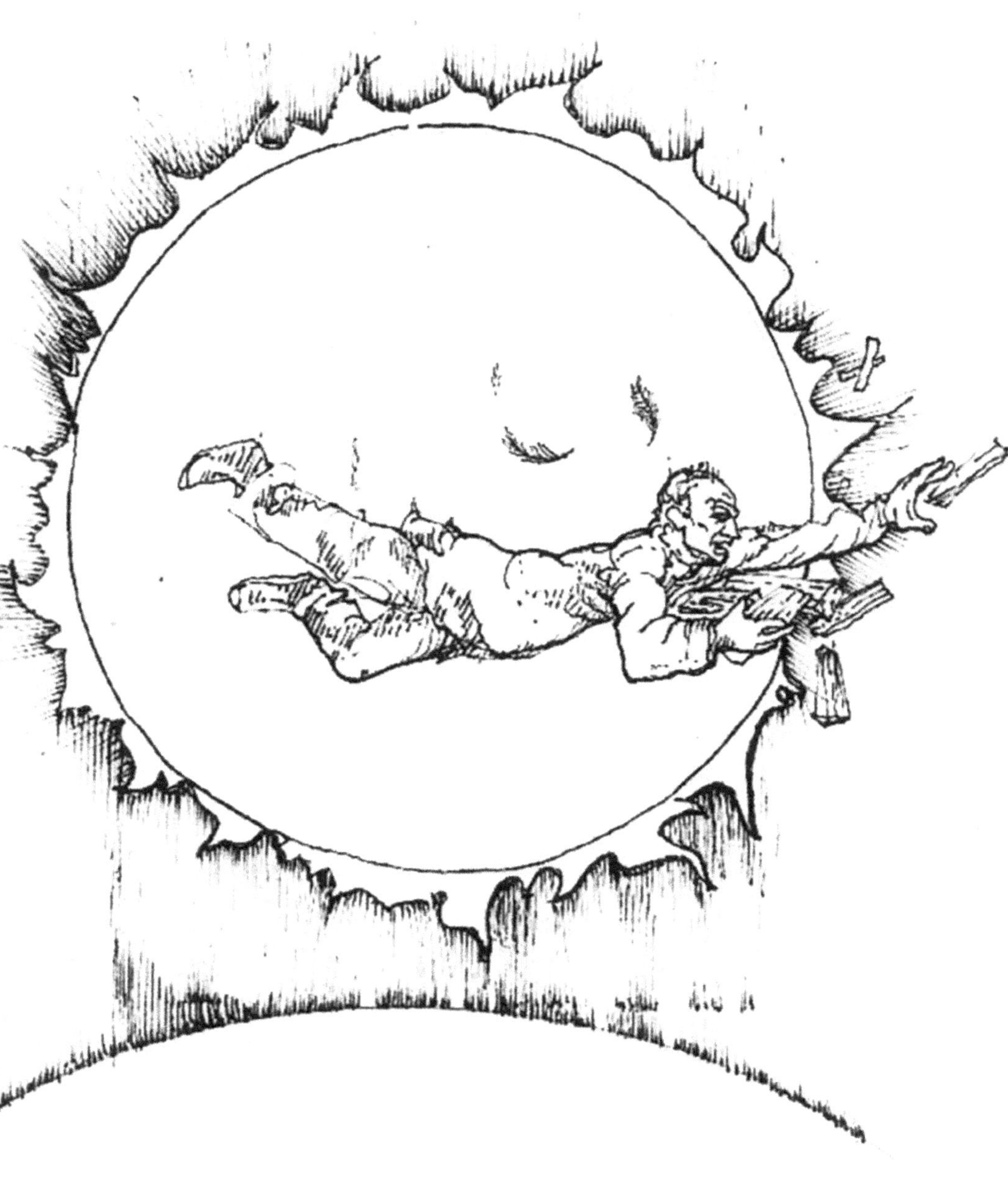

LIKE AN OLD MAN FALLING

the woman who doesn't talk
speaks to the whole neighbourhood

the child who walks alone to
& from school is the most visible

this afternoon i fell with an armful
of firewood like an old man falling

EVERYDAY CHRIST

You spoke in tongues
in the spirit of a child
until the Songs
of Experience chimed.

You sweat old crimes,
romance the past,
lavish relationships
that didn't last.

You're one of the many
hidden in plain sight
with the flesh & blood
of an Everyday Christ.

There's talk of End Times
but that's nothing new,
shocking, benign, it'll
come calling for you.

HOME

Home, happy, laying on a bed
witnessing trees in breeze, in light

wondering who lay here before? Who
planted the blue gum, laid the stone wall?

Why did they plant an Australian tree,
rather than a native? Did the action come

with a dedication? Why am I happy today
when yesterday I felt jaded, mildly tainted?

Home sweet, home sour; so much relates,
down to the milk's use-by date.

CHOCOLATE-COLOURED CAT

I'm up in the wee hours. It being a balmy night
the doors & windows are open. I work intuitively.
At 2.30 I call time quietly. Entering my bedroom
I'm greeted by a chocolate-coloured cat on the bed.
I tickle under her chin, she felinely circles my hand.
I slip into bed, she furls into the folds of my legs.

When I wake at 7 she's on the pillow beside me.
She pushes her wet nose into my cheek.
When I get up, she curls into the space
I've left & when I return she's gone.
I place my hand down to where she's been;

feel the warmth.

HELLO

The old Scottish lady
who lives in
the pensioner flats
down the road
calls me sweetie
& I call her dear.

Every so often
we meet & greet
& go our own ways.
We've learnt that
nature abhors
a needy neighbour.

HUSH PUPPIES

Patti Smith owns a pair of Pope Benedict's slippers;
also a pair of Robert Mapplethorpe's.

I buy a new pair of slip-ons, Hush Puppies,
from Hannahs at Coastlands.

Outside the mall I discreetly slip the old pair
into a rubbish bin, & with a new spring

in my step comes an image
of an ice shelf, of an ice shelf calving.

AT CAFE 6

I've found the sweet spot.
'Capturing all the sun,' he cracks.
Like me, he's wearing a flat hat,
the sort worn by Andy Capp,

except mine's blue, his black,
he with his sunfrocked wife,
me alert & sun-lit like
a lone prairie wolf.

Attracting attention,
I shift from my seat
to one in a shady position;
even with a flat hat

there's a limit to the heat
a bloke can take.

A KIND OF PRIEST

Sun & sky reflect in tidal puddles,
Wee dog looks at Bill, then at the stick

'People don't want to hear my troubles.
They regard me as a kind of priest.'

Bill flicks the stick, wee dog runs after it.
'So I've learnt to listen, nod & breathe.'

ON MY 71st BIRTHDAY

Went to the supermarket.
Did a lap of the block.

Tinkered under the bonnets
of a couple of poems.

Steered into space.
All go!

Light & Shadow

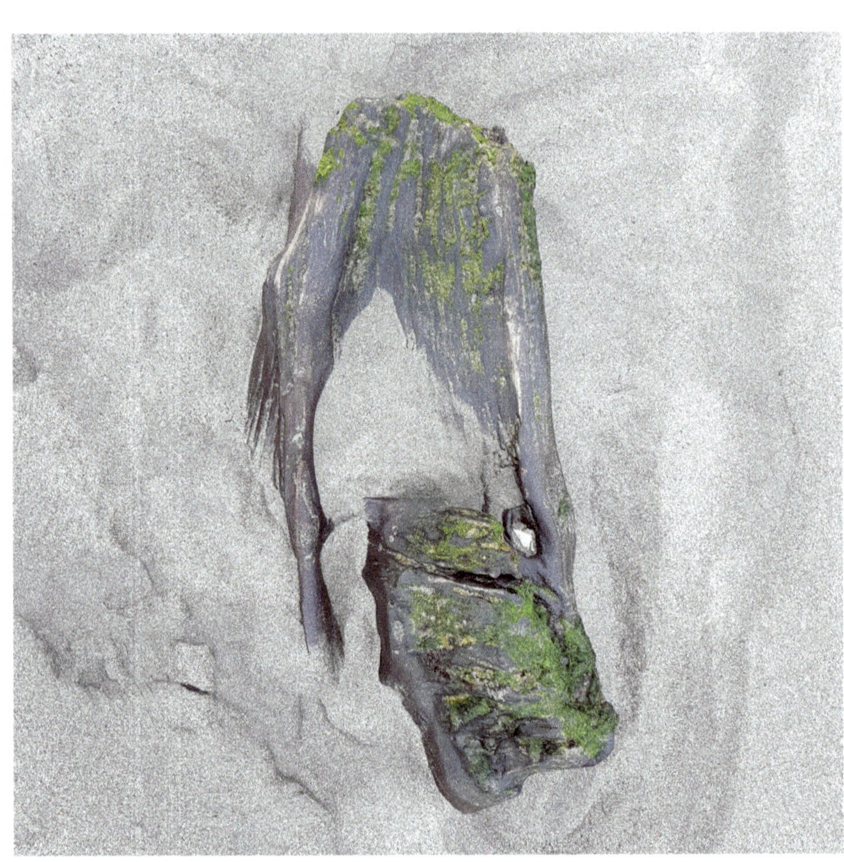

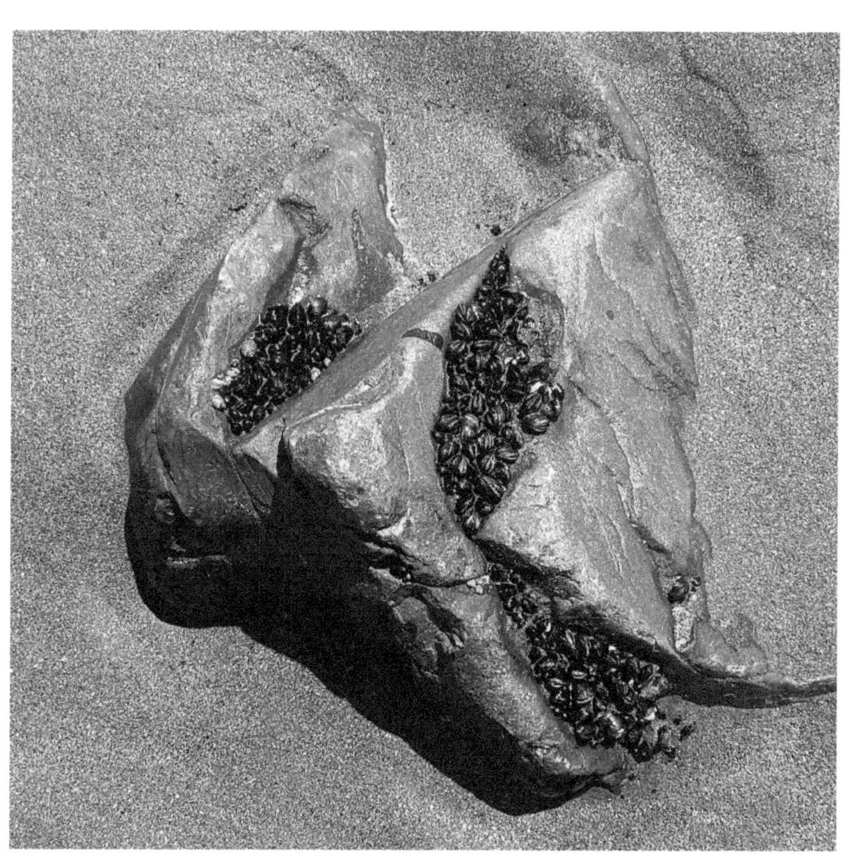

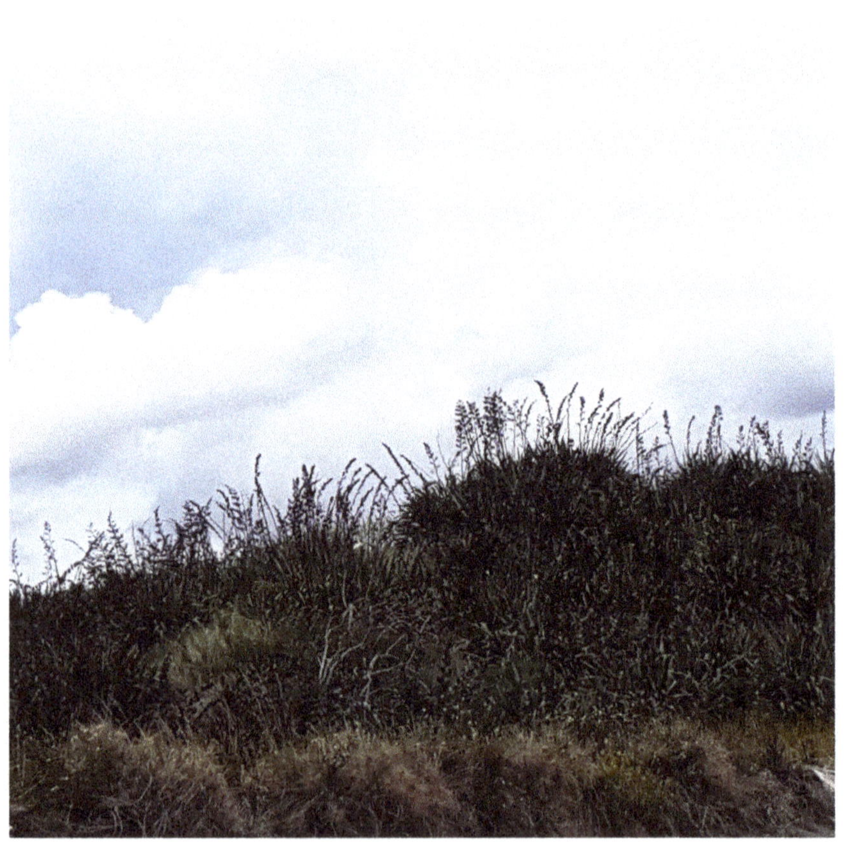

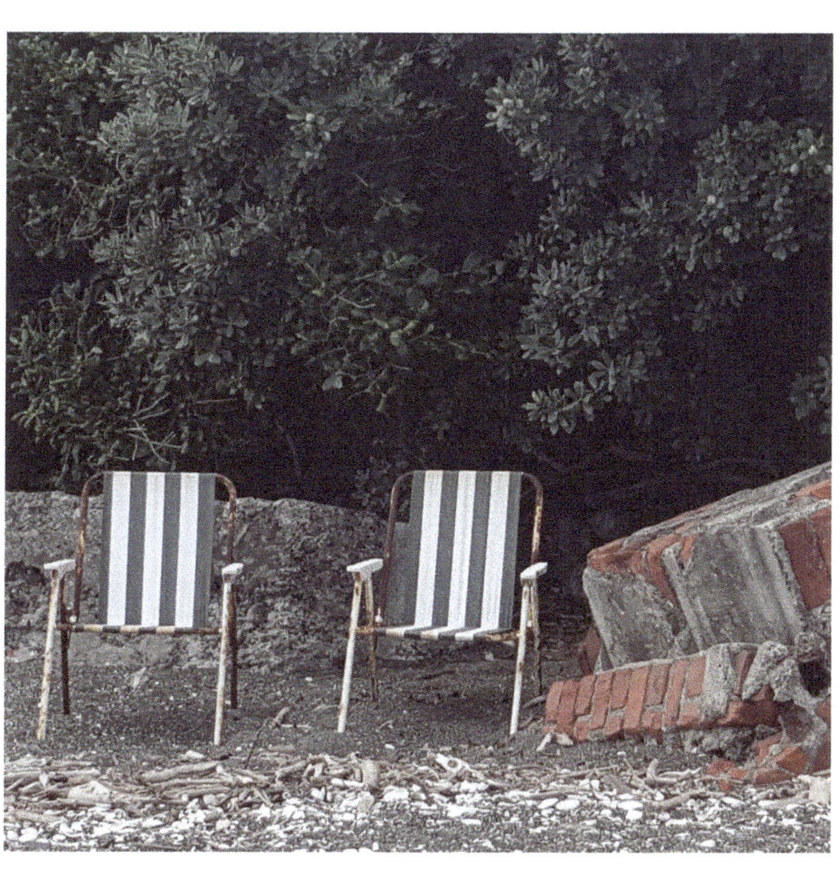

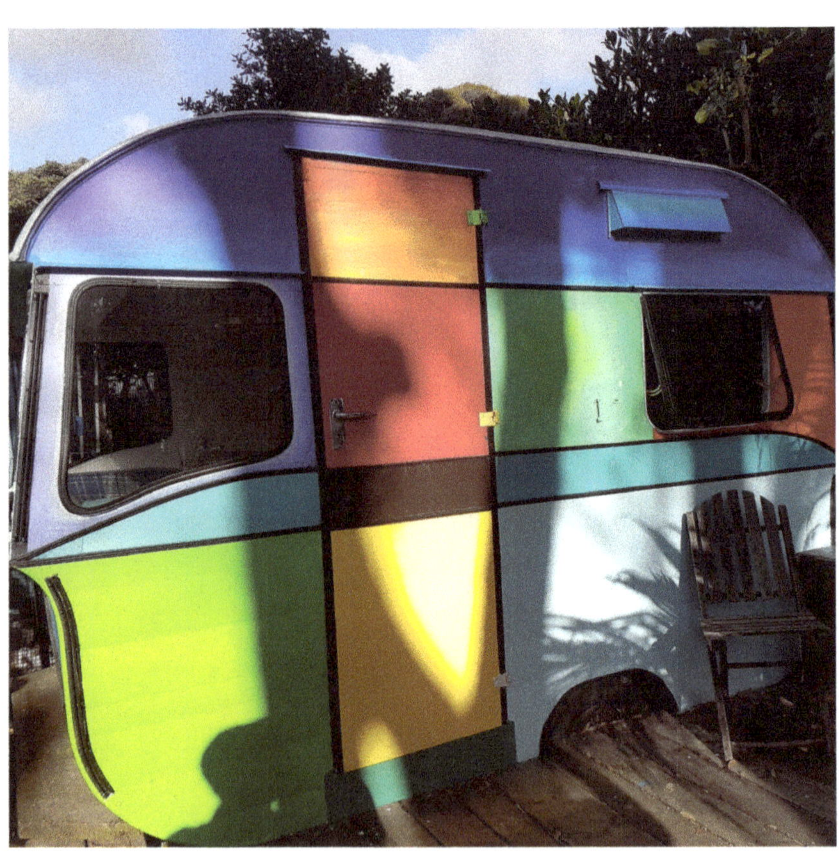

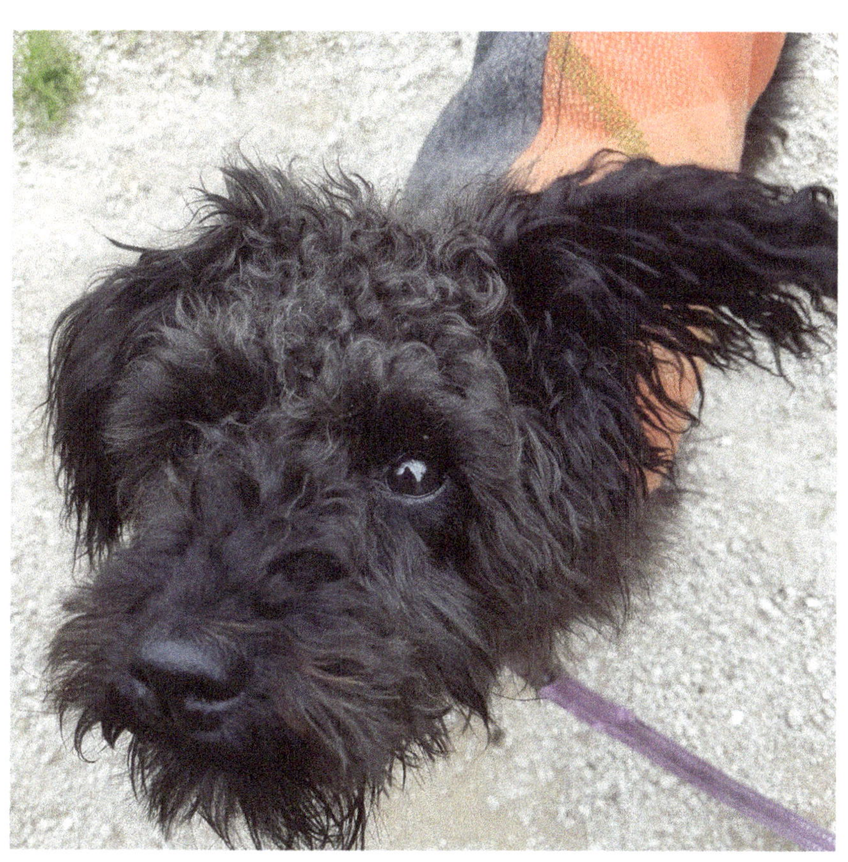

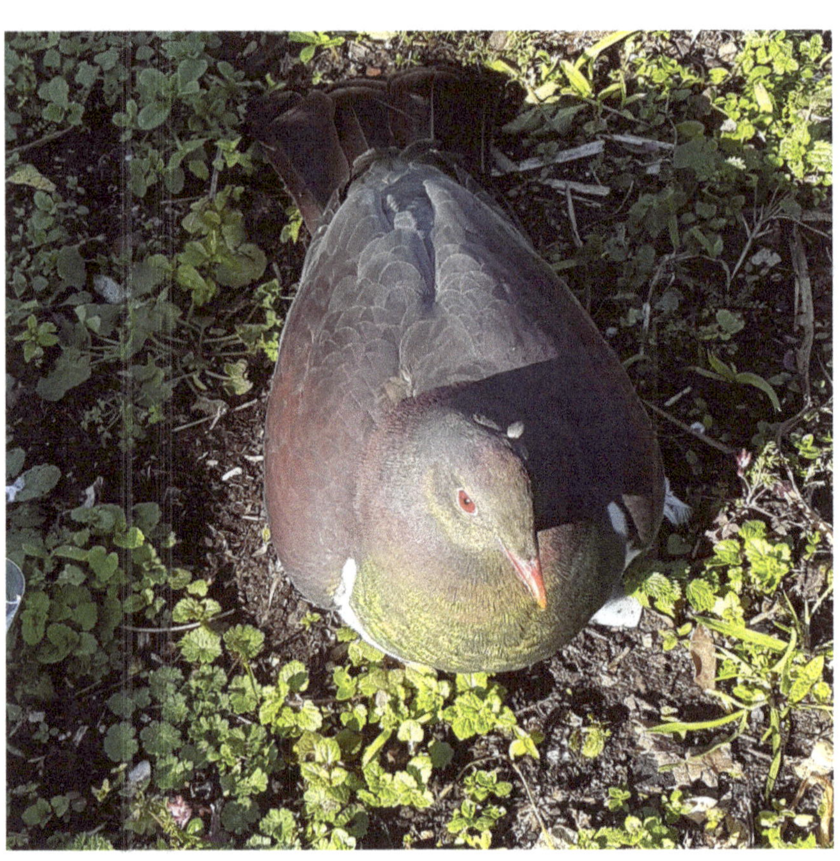

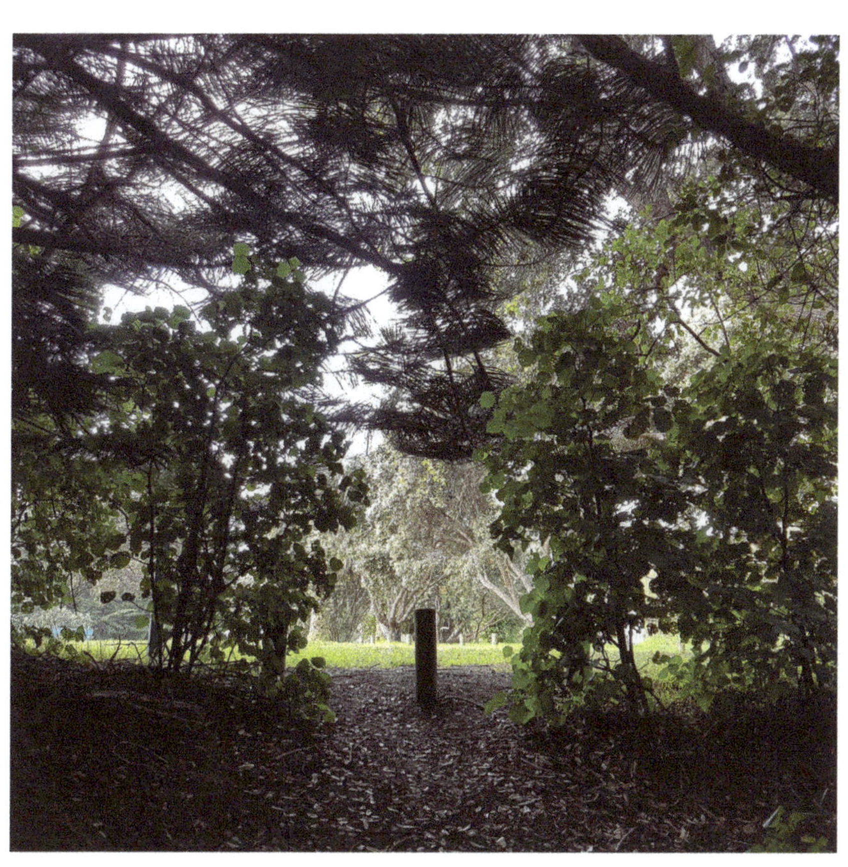

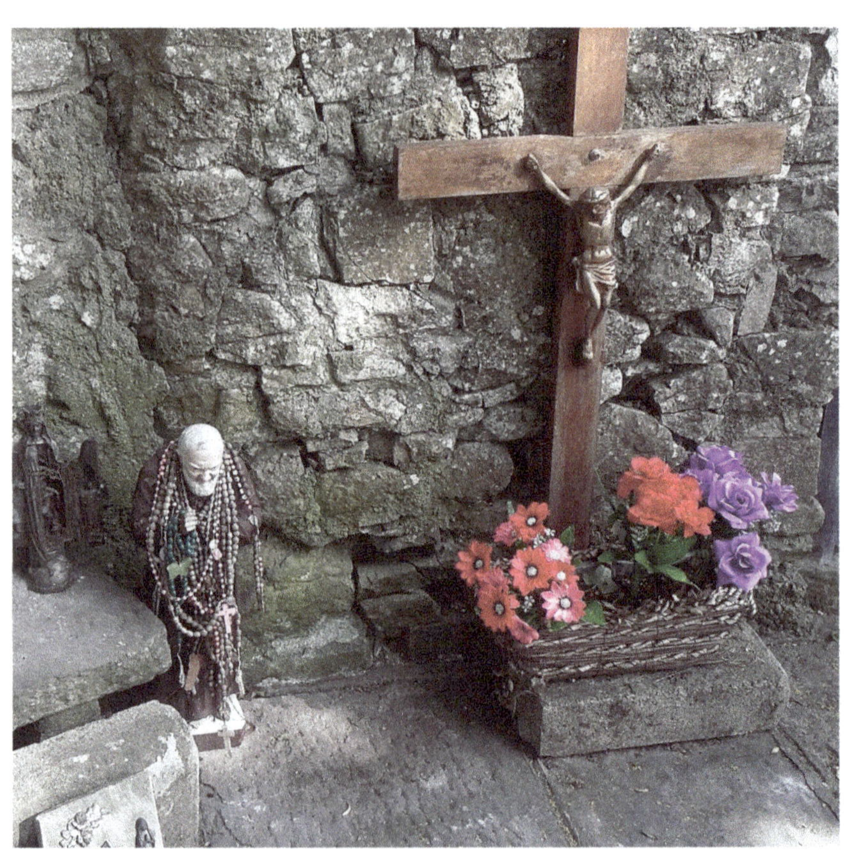

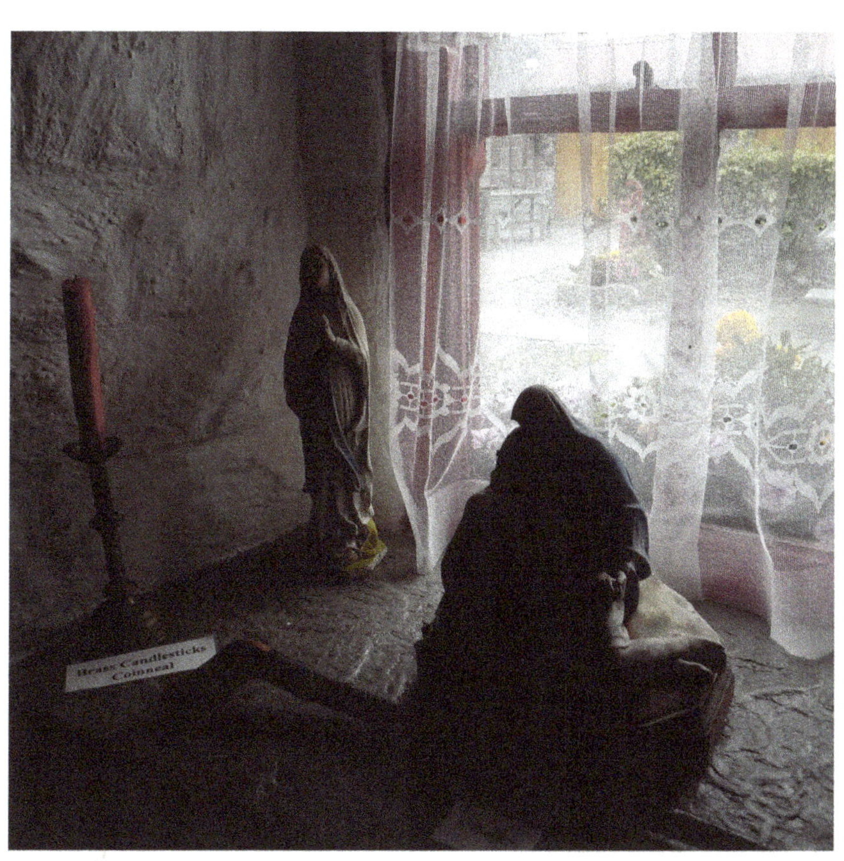
Brass Candlesticks
Coinneal

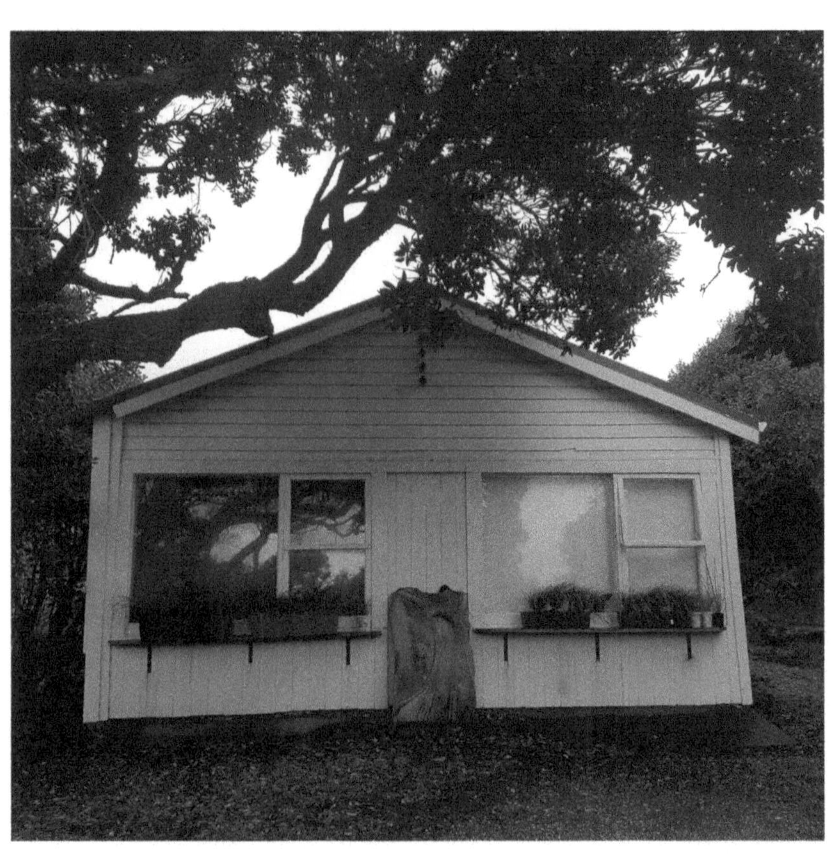

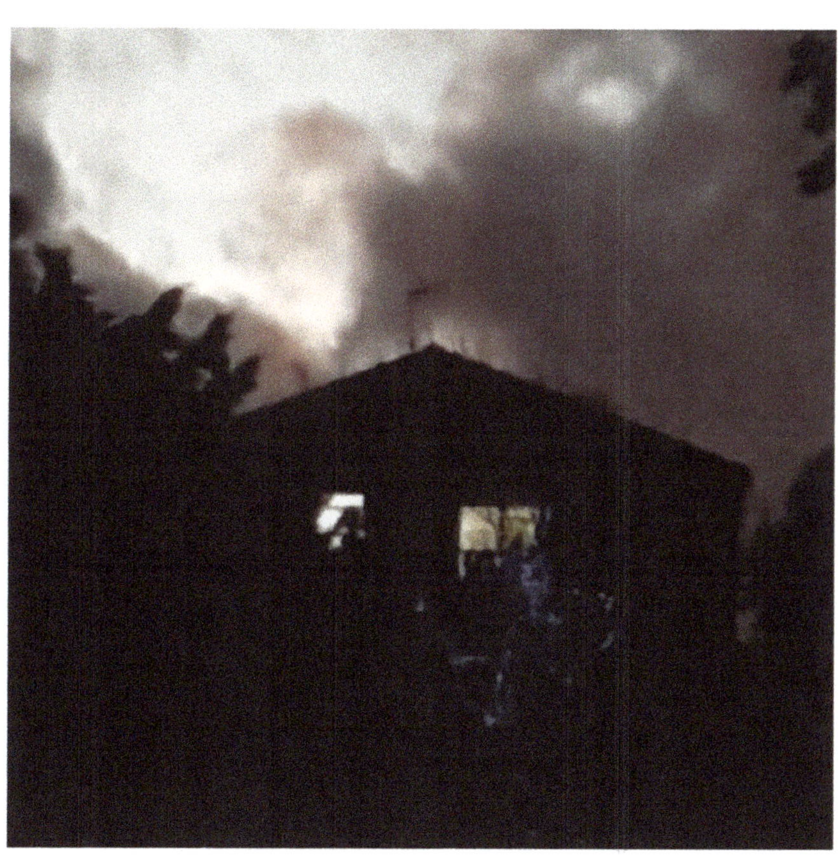

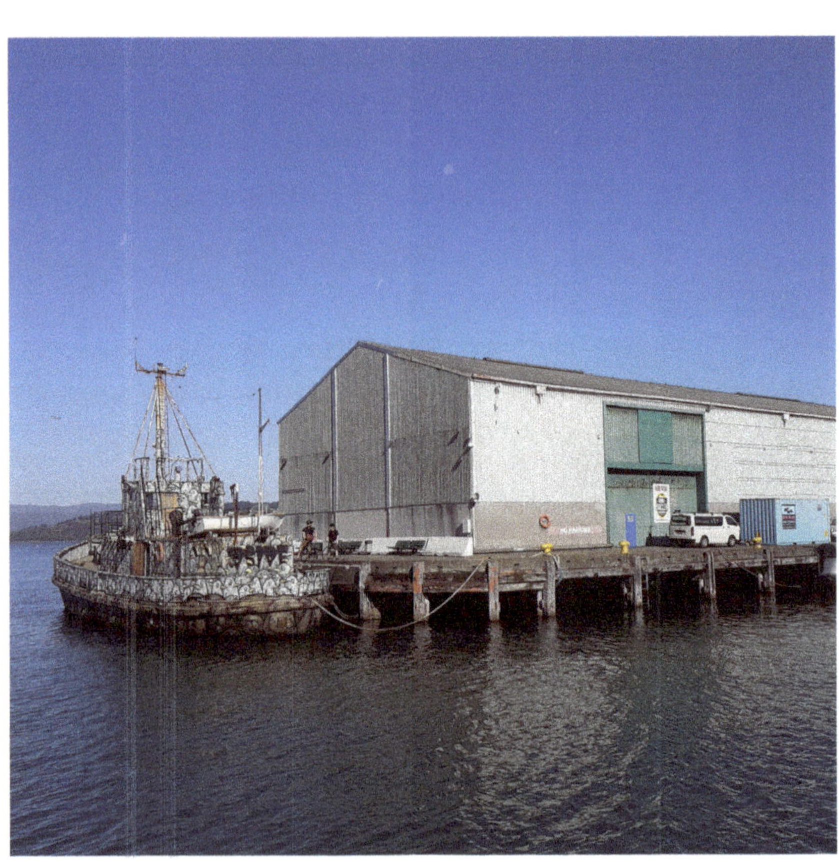

New & Uncollected Poems

Karma

Born to them
These cries
This quietude

This evening
This morning
This afternoon

Tomorrow
Born out of
Yesterday

One's life
Lived in light
And shadow

Boomer Consumer

May

I look forward to wearing my winter clothes
I'll treat myself to a new winter coat
From an upmarket menswear shop
Wear it home on the train
Feeling good about myself

November

I look forward to wearing my summer clothes
I'll treat myself to a new Hawaiian shirt
From an outlet with *je na sais quoi*
Wear it strolling the waterfront
Looking colourful, cotton scented

Fruitless

Going through my stuff
finding what I thought lost

but not what I'm looking for
leaves me wistful

over that gone world
this nevermore

strewn from banana boxes
to the livingroom floor

Out in the Cold

Darkness licks you
with a ghostly tongue.

You shiver like a German soldier
in a Russian winter.

In the dark & the cold,
& a long way from home.

Dug in

'We're well dug in,'
says the Ukrainian officer

in sight of the Russians.
'Shelling's at night,

& it's intensive.
They think they can out-gun us

but they can't;
nor can they move around us.'

Dug in sounds 20th century;
all soldiers die eventually.

Lest we forget, they repeat,
turning in their graves.

Brokenhearted

He buries her in the crater
Made by the missile
Instrumental in killing her

Rain

drops on the white trellis
& the bougainvillaea's
papery scarlet flowers

drops with a plink
plonk plink on
the wheelbarrow

the sweet
wet earth smells
an earthy prayer

Colour Blind

My mind cannot accept
That blue is Democrat
And red is Republican

Like the white woman
Married to the black judge
Cannot accept the election

Wasn't stolen. Like those
God-fearing folk sending
Greenbacks to a charlatan

Carl Jung

Was a man with beady eyes
And an animal warmth

Carl Jung
Was a famous analyst
Who lived by a lake

Carl Jung
Was in his time
Before his time

Carl Jung
Created history
Collecting herstory

Carl Jung
Built his house
Storey by story

Sleepwalker

My Chinese sneakers leak. They cost 15 bucks
at The Warehouse. I didn't seek poverty.
It found me grizzling on Renown Road.

It found me shivering on the Russian Steppes.
As a kid I sleepwalked. My night wandering
became legend. I trekked to slums & to palaces.

I sleepwalked to my grandparents' house.
They found me in the gold room.
They found me in the bed without sheets.

A Man of Letters

'I am going to be a man
of letters,' I tell my parents.
I am 18 years old.

They look at each other,
then at me, & laugh!
'Shall I reacquaint you
with your school reports?'
my mother asks.

I read them Get Drunk! –
a poem by Baudelaire.
His words thud & clang
on my clumsy tongue.

'Isn't it great,' my father says,
'that simple folk like us
could have bred a genius!'

New Friend

My mother's made a new friend at the rest home:
'She's 100 years old & still has her marbles.
It's good, I have someone to talk to.'

'Oh, there she goes now;
on her way out for a cigarette.'

Thought of You

from being alive
to being dead to living
brightly in my head

Life Lesson

We had parents
With problems
They did their best
So we forgave them

White Silence

You've overstepped, misread
the terrain, yet stumble on . . .
in trouble, troubled, a whimpered
prayer nags at your fear.

You're that Nietzschean figure
in an alpine winter
with a waning belief
in an interventionist God.

Shadows tail shadows,
jag rocks, then a crack,
a deep rumble, rumbling
to a white silence.

Loping up the slope,
a Saint Bernard Dog.

Sketch

Kapiti Island lies
regally off the coast;
once used & abused,
now a sanctuary to life.

Storm-tides have left
a scatter of driftwood
washed from along
the Taranaki Bight;

a pair of gulls feed
on snapper's eyes,
wade & ride
the tail-end surf;

walking the beach
an old Maori man,
mokopuna in hand,
nods & smiles.

The Good Shepherd

Lamb chops for dinner?
With garlic & olive oil,
rosemary & thyme for flavour?

Me? I'm just trying
to stay alive as long
as meaning lasts,

as long as a painting by
Pieter Brueghel the Younger:
holds its blood-lust hunger.

Fashioner

Meet me
From a long way off

Meet me
Through seamist

Meet me
By lapping water

Meet me
With vigour's blush

Meet me
With a storyline

Meet me
With a soulful song

Pastiche

The cosmic tribe's *shopping for images*
At the Galactic Supermarket:

Geoff Cochrane's grinning at a baby,
While Leonard Cohen charms its mother.

By the fruit and veg Nick Cave's
Chatting with Marianne Faithfull,

And lo . . . here comes the Maori Jesus
Rapping the song of himself in te reo.

On the bus I catch the Ratana Brass Band
Playing outside a halfway house on Rimu Road;

Getting off I'm greeted by the ghost of Hemi
Baxter, his face *wrinkled with the tribal smile.*

Hey Man

Why talk so harshly?
You become what you utter.
Bitter. Unbecoming.

Vicious judgements
Don't serve you well,
Eh, man?

Tell us a soulful story
We're here, all ears.

Linkage

All words have
A following

Say to
Blackbirds

Philosophy
Or cage fighting

Ask what you will
You'll get a reaction

Awake or asleep
Especially asleep

Talking thru
Broken teeth.

Anxiety Dream

On the cold streets
Of gothic Invercargill
In a nightshirt
Like Mad King George

Sweeping Trill

Mistaking
a nesting starling's
harsh trill

for the scratch, scratch
of a neighbour's
sweep, sweeping,

I gut, gut
chuckle
while the cat's

ears muscle
muscle at
thicket rustle.

Bird or rodent?
What's heard
in a moment

is lost in a moment.
Squawk, squawk,
rustle, rustle.

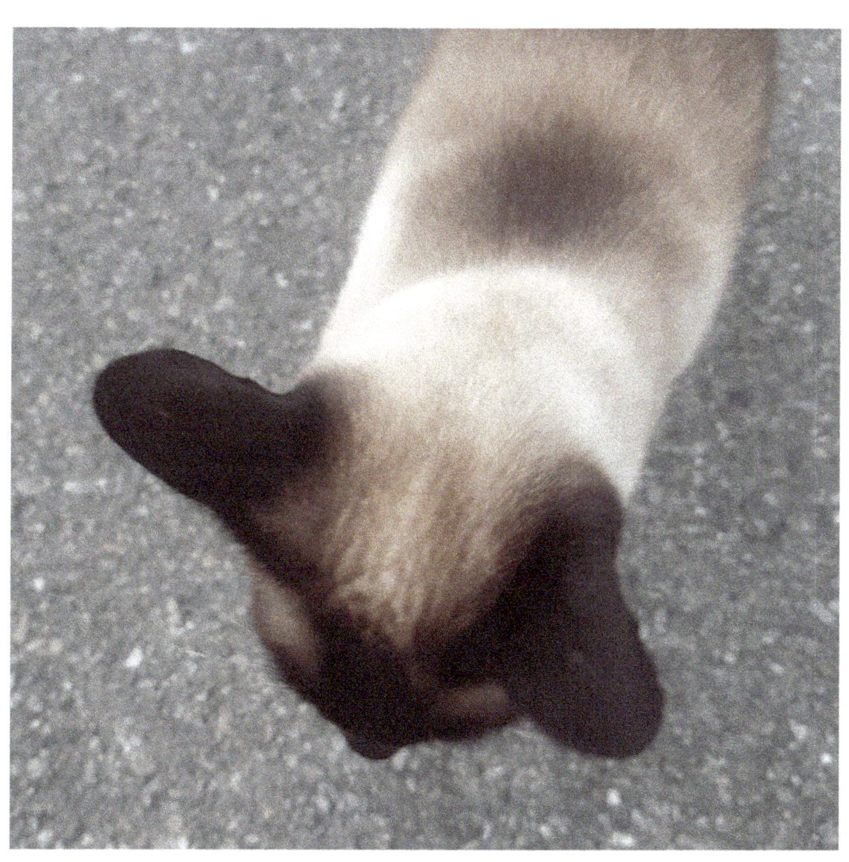

Bibliography

Poetry

upagainstit, Voice Press, 1983. The poem *a Hockney pool* published in Landfall 146; *letter from holloway road* selected by editors Gregory O'Brien & Louise St John for the anthology *Big Weather, Poems of Wellington,* first published by Mallinson & Rendel Publishers Ltd, 2000; revised edition published by Penguin Random House New Zealand, 2018.

ON THE LINE (with drawings by Jane Pountney) Voice Press, 1985. The segment beginning *music sounds* published in the NZ Listener.

thewayofit (with drawings by Jane Pountney) Black Robin Press, 1988. The poem *a way* was integrated into the multi-panelled charcoal work entitled *Towards A Landscape* by Jane Pountney, first exhibited at the Southern Cross Gallery (aka the Gregory Flint Gallery), Wellington, then at the Christina Barton-curated group show *After McCahon* at Auckland City Gallery in 1988; *shifting points* was selected by editor Jenny Bornholdt for the anthology *Short Poems of New Zealand*, Victoria University Press, 2018.

SET PIECE, Hutcheson Bowman & Stewart (printers), 1988. Produced as a type catalogue.

Prayers for the Living & the Dead (with drawings by Bodhi Vincent), Voice Press, 2021. The poems *Day of the Dead, The Beats, Nano Sleeps, Bob & Hello* published in the NZ Listener; *Delivery & Hush Puppies* in Landfall; *Flowers* in Poetry New Zealand Poetry Yearbook, *Helen 1962-2012* in the Australian online literary magazine Cordite.

Prose

These Lives I Have Buried, Four Winds Press, 2004, as part of the Lloyd Jones-edited Montana Estates Essay series.

Exhibitions

BODY SHAPE, photo/poem, Alexandra Public Library, 1990. The poem *a gain* from **thewayofit** was integrated with family photos for the multi-panelled work. It was redesigned for Landfall 178; the title photo appeared on the magazine's cover.

SET PIECE, silkscreen prints, BAM, Wellington Public Library, 1996.

Album

This 'I', Waiata and the Word, 2011.

Author's Notes

A number of years after Jane and I parted ways in 1993 - her to her life, me to a drug and alcohol rehabilitation centre in the Rangitikei - I broached with her the possibility of an interdisciplinary treatment of *One The Line*. She was in favour of the idea, and now, as well as reprinting the little book in this volume, movements are afoot to do just that.

Jane, gone two decades this year, as well as being a gifted painter, was well loved by her students. During the eight years that we were married, she worked as an art teacher for the Correspondence School; a prolific letter writer, she hand wrote to her students, gallery curators, art dealers, colleagues, family and friends, that included my mother's eldest brother Gordon, a painter and sculptor. She also sent him invites, catalogues and reviews of our collaborative work and her solo shows, which he diligently archived. I inherited the hefty folder, along with a clutch of his artworks.

Gordon was an early influence; I'd peruse his art books, delight in his art practice, and the objects in which he found beauty, such as the old farm machinery, out of which he made his sculptural assemblages. In turn he was quick to write in praise of my first little book *upagainstit*, designed by poet and craft printer Alan Loney, another influence, who also did the original design work for *On The Line* and *thewayofit*.

My gratitude is also due to the Lasavia team: Mike Johnson, Rowan Johnson and Daniela Gast for their parts in the making of this book.

About the Author

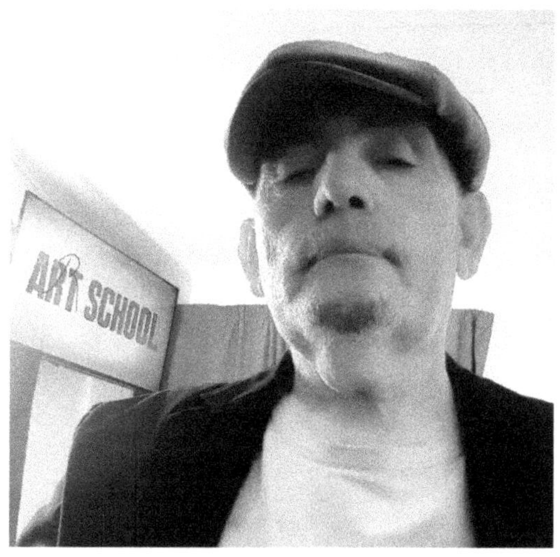

Lindsay Rabbitt was born in Invercargill, Aotearoa New Zealand's southernmost city, in 1950, and raised under the big skies of Central Otago, home district of his mother's maternal people. As a young man he trained as a hand and machine typographer and worked for newspapers and commercial printing houses. In the 1980s he purchased a Wellington typesetting and graphic design business. Renaming it Voice Press, he published poetry and short fiction. He reinvented himself as a journalist in the 1990s, working as a reporter/sub-editor for the *Kapiti Observer*, later writing (freelance) artist profiles, radio and book reviews for the *NZ Listener*. He occasionally writes book reviews for *Landfall Review Online*. He has lived on the Kapiti Coast for almost three decades and performs his poems with the song and spoken word troupe Waiata & the Word.

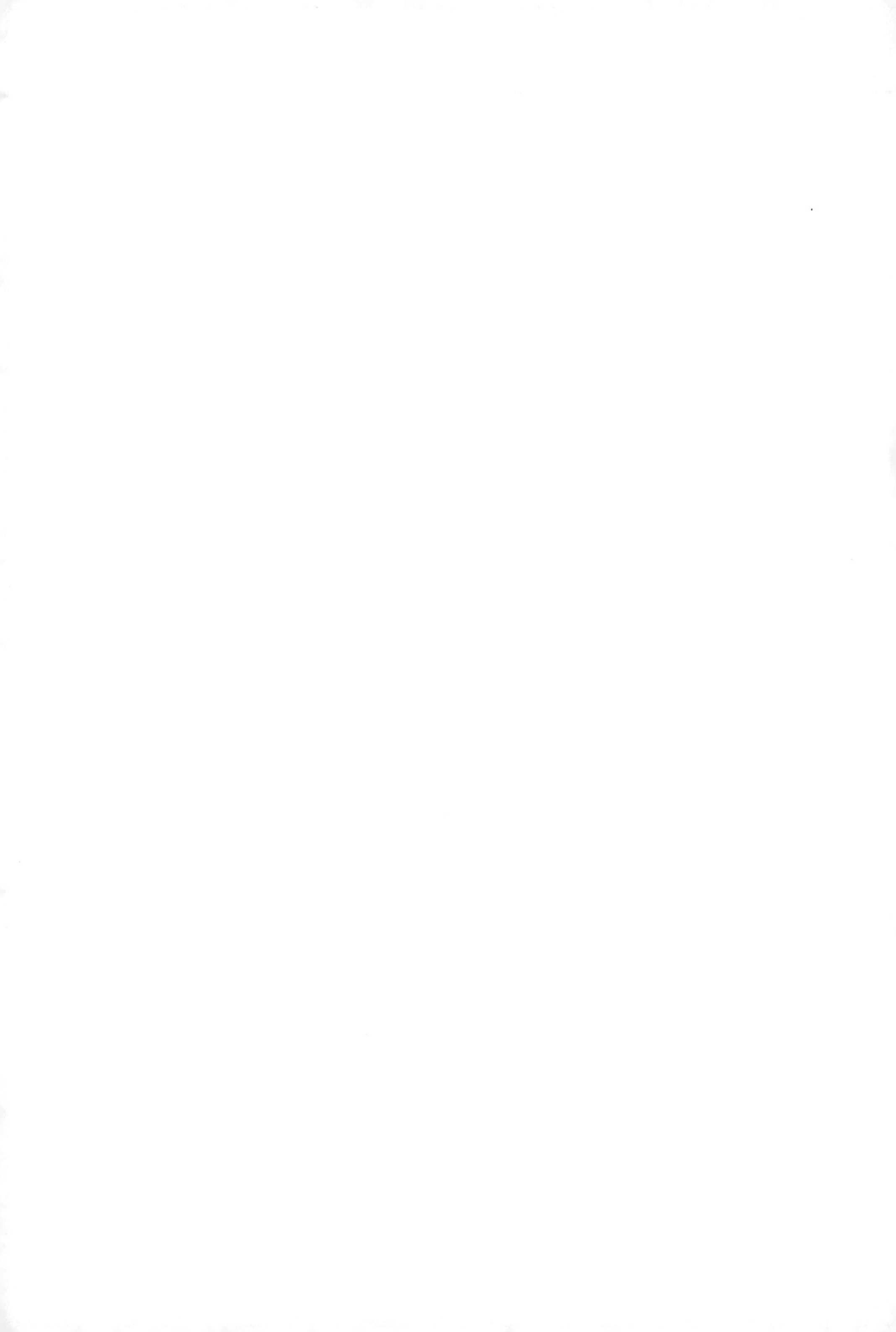

www.ingramcontent.com/pod-product-compliance
Lightning Source LLC
Chambersburg PA
CBHW050026040726
47599CB00015B/1558